MENTAL
SNACKS™

Nourishment for your mind and fuel for your life!

JULIO MELARA

MENTAL SNACKS™

Nourishment for your mind and fuel for your life!

By

Julio A. Melara

Mental Snacks
ISBN 0-9642430-5-9
Cover Design by Hoa Vu

To order more copies of this book or for further information on Julio Melara, log on to www.juliomelara.com.

"What you dwell on,
you empower and enlarge.
Good always multiplies when you dwell
upon on it, but so does negativity.
The choice is yours.
Which do you want more of?"

—Julio A. Melara

To Hillary, Jonathan and Jordan

INTRODUCTION

We live in a fast paced world. Most of us are racing through our lives. The relentless demands of work, marriage, family, finances and even friendships can take their toll. Many folks seem to be just trying to get through the day.

This is why I wrote *Mental Snacks*.

I learned a long time ago that every battle we fight in life begins in the mind. In order for your outer world to change, your inner world must change first. We must be sure we are approaching life and all of its challenges in the right manner by renewing our minds daily.

Renewing your mind is a journey. We are all bombarded with negative thoughts daily - and that's why we need mental snacks. Inside this book, you'll find practical, down-to-earth insights to help you prepare for the battles of life. No matter what negative thoughts exist in your mind, you have the potential to move forward and experience the positive things God intended for your life. When you begin to focus on filling your mind with positive thoughts and the right perspective, it will bring freedom and peace to your life.

My hope is that as you digest these mental snacks, they will help you make necessary changes in your thinking and perspective. You have inside of you the potential to make a difference in your family, work and community—but it all starts with the way you think.

The mental snacks in this book were developed and learned over the last 25 years of my life. Some content reflects my learning from other books and lessons from mentors, friends and colleagues who have been influential in my development. This book can be read cover to cover one mental snack at a time or by subject matter. They will nourish your soul and fuel your life if you read them, believe them and apply them!

—*Julio*

GROWTH

P oet Robert Browning wrote, "Why do we stay on the earth except to grow?" Most people would agree that growing is a good thing, but relatively few people dedicate themselves to the process. Why? Because growth requires change, and most people are reluctant to change. The truth is that without change, growth is impossible. Growth demands a temporary surrender of security, getting out of your comfort zone. It may mean giving up familiar but limiting patterns, safe but unrewarding work, values no longer believed in, relationships that have lost their meaning. Most people do not realize that successful and unsuccessful people do not differ substantially in their abilities. The difference is in their desire to reach their potential. Nothing is more effective when it comes to reaching your potential than a commitment to personal growth!

Growing and Changing

Change your thoughts and change your life…behind everything you do, there's a thought!In the book of Proverbs, it says, "As a person thinks, so he or she is." So if you want to change your *life*, you have to change your *thinking*. Think about this:

Imagine riding in a speedboat with an automatic pilot set to go east. If you suddenly decide to head west, you've got two options: One is to grab the wheel and force it to head in the opposite direction from where it's programmed to go. By sheer willpower, you could overcome the autopilot, but you'd feel constant resistance. Your arms would eventually become fatigued, you'd let go of the wheel and guess what? The boat would instantly head back east because that's the way it's internally programmed to go.

That's what happens when you try to change your life through willpower. "I'll force myself to eat less, exercise more, quit being disorganized, etc." Yep, willpower can produce short-term change, but it creates constant stress because you haven't dealt with the root cause. The change doesn't feel natural, so eventually you give up, go off your diet, quit exercising and revert to your old patterns.

Thank God, there's a better way! The second option is to change your autopilot—the way you think! There's an ancient scripture that says, "Let God transform you into a new person by changing the way you think" (Rom. 12:2 NLT). Change always starts in your mind. The way you *think* determines the way you *feel*, and the way you *feel* determines the way you *act*. One of the keys is to have a personal growth plan.

Having a personal growth plan is a decision that will make the biggest difference in your life. Here are three simple principles that will help you develop into a person dedicated to personal growth:

1. Start by growing today.
Many people have the "someday sickness." They could do things to bring value to their lives today, but, instead, they put them off and say, "I will do it later or someday." The best way to success is to start today. Growth today is an investment for tomorrow.

2. Expose yourself to what is new.
If you are not learning every day, your competition is. Learn something new every day. New information is essential to your success. It helps you to acquire knowledge that replaces what is out of date, and it builds on what you learned yesterday. In today's fast-changing world, it's not so much what you know any more that counts, because often what you know is old. It's how fast you learn!

3. Don't be satisfied with your current achievements.
(Be content, but not satisfied.)
The old saying "The greatest enemy of tomorrow's success is today's success" is so true. Success is much more difficult to manage than failure. Once you have achieved success, the tendency is to sit back and enjoy it. You have to be persistent enough to realize that nothing stays the same. It either gets better or worse. No matter how much you have achieved or how much success you have experienced, don't allow yourself to get complacent. Stay hungry! Do not get stuck in the comfort zone or let success go to your head. Enjoy the fruits of your labor (go ahead and celebrate your successes), then move on to greater growth!

> "Nothing can stop the person with the right mental attitude from achieving their goal; nothing on earth can help the person with the wrong mental attitude."
> —Thomas Jefferson

FOCUS

One of the primary reasons many organizations and people don't reach the levels of success and productivity they desire is because their focus is broken. Focus is anything that consumes your time, energy, finances and attention. If you are going to have success in your career, marriage, health or any area of your life, you're going to have to decide and define what you want and then focus! Your focus determines your energy. It determines your mastery and your future. Fragmented or broken focus, on the other hand, destroys your dream. It creates an unending parade of tragedies and disasters in your life. For example, bad friendships or unfruitful relationships do not feed, fuel or fertilize your focus on your goals. Get rid of them. Be the gatekeeper of your eyes, ears and heart. In order to live your dreams, you have to unclutter your life and get rid of distractions so you can focus!

Staying Focused

Four great benefits to focused living are:

1. **It simplifies your life!** When you don't know your purpose, you try to do too much, which causes stress, fatigue, conflict and, in many cases, confusion. You only have enough time and energy to do the God-given assignments for your life. Not getting everything done might be an indicator that you're doing more than God intended you to do. Focused living leads to a simpler lifestyle and a saner schedule.

2. **You become effective by being selective.** Contrary to what many motivational gurus tell you, you cannot do everything! But you can do something. If you want your life to have impact, you must be focused. Don't confuse activity with productivity. Diffused light has limited impact, but when it's focused like a laser, it can cut through steel.

3. It motivates you. Nothing energizes and empowers you like a clear purpose. It is meaningless work, not overwork, that tears us down and wears us out. George Bernard Shaw wrote, "This is the true joy of life: being used for a purpose, recognized by yourself as a mighty one; being a force of nature instead of a selfish clot of ailments and grievances, complaining that the world will not devote itself to make you happy." To know whether something is worth doing, ask yourself these three questions:
1. Will it matter in five years?
2. Do I need it?
3. Can it help others?

4. It prepares you for eternity. People who spend their lives trying to create a lasting legacy on earth fail to recognize that all achievements are eventually surpassed, all records broken, all reputations fade and tributes are forgotten. Ultimately, what matters most is not what others say about you, but what your family and God says. So live with that in mind. Think long-term.

A life of purpose and fulfillment is not about hocus pocus, it's about focus!

"The best way to appreciate your job
is to imagine yourself without one."
—Oscar Wilde

WORK

I n a national survey of 180,000 American workers, 80% indicated a dislike for their jobs. It's a sad reflection on an activity that will absorb a major portion of our lives. To make matters worse, people who dislike their vocation will never qualify for promotion or financial rewards. Think about Thomas Edison's perspective on work. He said, "I never did a day's work in my life. It was all fun." He believed the purpose of work was joy and fulfillment. So how do you get beyond the feeling that your work is only enjoyable at lunch time and on payday? To start with, study what you are doing, like what you are doing and believe in what you are doing! Stop looking at work simply as a means of earning a living and start realizing it is one of the keys to making a life.

A few years ago I received a call inquiring about a speaking engagement. The caller shared with me how he had read about my career and the sales records I had achieved. In the middle of the conversation he asked me, "What are some of the keys to becoming a top producer?" Below, I share them with you today.

1. I loved and love what I do.
In business and in life you must have passion. You must be able to get excited about what you do. Passion is all about the attitude and energy you bring to the job every day! Having a passion for what you do will not only help you get through the tough times but also qualifies you for promotion and success. Think about this for a moment. When the name Thomas Edison is mentioned, you think inventions. When the name Henry Ford is mentioned, you think automobiles. When you hear Tiger Woods, golf comes to mind. Bill Gates, software. Every one of these people possessed a passion for their job. When people mention your name, what do they say? What are you known for in your industry?

2. I studied my trade.
You must become a student of your industry. You must make a

lifetime commitment to learning. Remember, it doesn't matter how old or how young you are. How long you've been in the business or how new you are to it. How much success you've had or how much you haven't had. You still have plenty to learn. How do I know? Simple answer. You can never exhaust your capacity to grow and learn. What are you doing on a daily basis to become a better leader? One of the most important lessons we all have to remember is that you have to renew your mind daily. Research currently shows that the average person has 40,000 thoughts a day and 80% of them are negative. What's going into your mind on a daily basis? What are you studying and applying on a consistent basis? Here is the key: Your work may be finished some day but not your education!

3. **I knew my customers and was committed to serving them.**
Unfortunately, in today's marketplace there's a rampant disease that is going around. It's become an epidemic. It's called the ME-ITIS…are you familiar with it? People only interested in their *own* interests! However, if you are going to have long-term success, your attitude has to be: How can I serve? How can I serve my customers? How can I serve my family? How can I serve my community? The concept is a simple one: If you want help, help others. If you want excellence, give excellence. If you want love, give it away. If you want a great team, be a great teammate. And if you want to be a leader in your company, community or industry, learn to serve. If you were arrested today and charged with, "being a leader on the team with a good attitude who serves others," would there be enough evidence to convict you?

4. **I focused!**
I believe the No. 1 reason companies and individuals do not reach their level of productivity, results, profits or success is because of broken focus. If you are going to accomplish your mission, you're going to have to un-clutter your life, get rid of distractions and focus!Some areas that deserve your focus are:

1. Giving value first to customers
2. Building and cultivating long-term relationships
3. Time and energy management
4. Health and fitness
5. Daily gratitude

"In this world of give and take, there are not
enough people willing to give what it takes."
—Unknown

COMMITMENT

Leaders, inventors, business people, dreamers, aspiring professionals and anyone else desiring to achieve and succeed in their endeavors must understand that the first step is to make a commitment to invest their life and talents toward all pursuits deserving their best efforts. What you commit yourself to be, will change who you are and make you into a different person. What are your commitments today? Where are you going? Who are you going to be? Show me a person who hasn't decided, and I'll show you someone who has no identity, no personality and no direction. Remember, a total commitment is paramount to reaching your ultimate goal!

Enough Lip Service

If you study the top achievers in any field, you will discover that they all have one central attribute—self-discipline.

But what exactly is self-discipline?

Self-discipline is nothing more than learning to control your impulses and delay short-term gratification for greater long-term rewards. It puts your money where your mouth is. Self-discipline begins where "lip service" ends. You may be self-motivated by desire. You may expect to become a CEO. You may feel you are in control. You may even imagine yourself going to the moon one day. But without self-discipline, you will not get off the launching pad. Anything you want to do well, you must do often. Whatever skill or quality you want to perfect, you must practice. That is where self-discipline enters the picture.

Self-discipline makes possible countless hours of practice, which lead to mastery. Self-discipline is different from habit. Self-discipline gives birth to habits, and habits create a future you will love or hate. Any person who wants to become a leader in his or her industry must understand the power of habit. Habit is a gift from God. It simply means anything you do twice becomes easier. You will never change your life until you change something you do daily. That may mean changing what you eat, how early you get out of bed or get to work, what you read or watch on television, and even what you say. What you are going to be tomorrow, you are becoming today. Psychologists say that when you perform an act for 21 days in a row, without fail, it will become a habit. Of course, self-discipline is not easy, but it pays big dividends. That's why you have to be committed to your goals!

Here are three steps to increase your commitment to succeed:

1. **Anticipate the rewards and count the cost.** Be aware of the sacrifices and challenges involved in realizing your goals, but focus on the rewards of success.
2. **Learn everything you can about your goal.** Read books and magazines so you understand as much as possible about your chosen profession.
3. **Constantly remind yourself of your dreams.** Strive continually to activate, nurture and maintain the kind of commitment that will help you achieve your goals. In any worthwhile endeavor, the ultimate victory goes to the person with the strongest commitment.

GROWING

A teacher with 25 years of experience and a new college graduate both applied for the same job. When the new graduate got the job, the experienced teacher demanded to know why. The superintendent said, "It may be true that you have 25 years' experience, but after checking your record, I discovered that you only taught for one year and repeated it for the next 24!" It is not how much time you put in—it's what you put into the time that counts. Everybody has experiences; the difference is some go through them and others grow through them. You must grow and learn every day. Don't stop growing and don't just recycle what you learned years ago. Your mind is the drawing board for tomorrow's circumstances. You will never be promoted until you become overqualified for your present position.

It Starts with Your Attitude

How's your attitude today? Your attitude not only affects who you are today, but also directs your future. The choices you have made up to now are the results of your attitude. Your attitude determines your actions, and your actions determine your achievements. The person you are and where you are today is the result of your attitude. How you think affects your life. Attitude gives us the power to become who we want to become, and determines who others think we are. You are who you are, and what you are because of the diversity of the thoughts in your mind. Proverbs 23:7 says, "As a person thinks, so he or she is." This is why attitude is so important.

I love what former UCLA head basketball coach John Wooden said, "Things turn out the best for the people who make the best of the way things turn out."

If I could share only one thing that I possess, it would be my attitude. My attitude, more than anything else, has helped me on my success journey. A positive attitude has always been my greatest asset, and it can be yours, too. Your attitude toward life determines life's attitude toward you.

Some people see the positive in every situation, while others go through life seeking their induction into the negative attitude hall of fame. Attitude is not everything, but it's the main thing!

How do you get and maintain a positive attitude? Here are some tips:

1. Renew your mind daily with positive information and education. (Read books or listen to them on CD).
2. Associate with positive and successful people.
3. Speak positively. Don't use words carelessly.
4. Live in the present. Maximize the moment.
5. Be thankful every day you wake up and are alive!
6. Don't take yourself too seriously—have fun!

> "Happiness cannot be traveled to, owned, learned, worn or consumed. Happiness is the spiritual experience of living every minute with love, grace and gratitude."
> —Denis Waitley

GRATITUDE

D o you have an attitude of gratitude or are you a constant complainer? Here is a morning prayer a friend sent me years ago that you should remember: "Even though I clutch my blanket and growl when the alarm goes off, thank you that I can hear—*there are many who are deaf.* Even though I close my eyes as long as possible against the morning light, thank you that I can see—*there are many who are blind.* Even though I huddle in my bed and put off the effort to rise, thank you that I have the strength to get up—*there are many who are bedridden.* Even though the first hour of my day is hectic, when socks are lost, toast is burned and tempers are short, thank you for my family—*there are many who are all alone.* Even though our breakfast never looks like the pictures in the magazines and the menu at times is limited, thank you for the food we have—*there are many who are hungry.* Count your blessings every day, for there are many who won't make it through the day."

Don't Take Life for Granted

On top of the Capitol dome in Washington, D.C., is a 20-foot statue of the "Freedom Lady." Her face is framed in a crest of stars, and she's holding a shield of stars and stripes in her hand. She was shipped from Rome, and during a fierce storm the captain ordered some cargo thrown overboard. The sailors wanted to ditch the "Freedom Lady," but the captain refused, shouting above the wind, "Never! We'll flounder before we throw freedom away!" Ben Franklin said, "Those who give up liberty for safety deserve neither liberty nor safety!" A wise man once said, "If we value anything more than freedom, we'll lose our freedom. And if we value comfort or money more, we'll lose those too."

In 1945 Martin Niemoeller said, "When the Nazis came for the Communists, I didn't speak up because I wasn't a Communist. When they came for the Jews, I didn't speak up because I wasn't a Trade Unionist. When they came for the Catholics, I didn't speak up because I was a Protestant. Then they came for me and, by that time, there was no one left to speak up for anybody."

We must guard against apathy, and never forget that much of the world doesn't enjoy the political and religious freedoms we take for granted. The opportunities to vote, worship and engage in the free enterprise system are all reasons to be thankful daily!

Grateful for Today

Did you know there are two days in every week that you should neither worry about nor fear? One of these days is yesterday, with its mistakes, its aches and pains, its faults and blunders. Yesterday has passed forever beyond your control. All the money in the world cannot bring back yesterday. You cannot erase a single word—yesterday is gone. The other day you should not worry about is tomorrow, with its large promise and possible burdens. Tomorrow is also beyond your immediate control. Tomorrow's sun will rise, either in splendor or behind a mask of clouds—but it will rise. You have no stake in tomorrow, because it hasn't arrived yet. This leaves only one day—today! Anybody can fight the battle of just one day. It is only when you take on the burdens of yesterday and tomorrow that you break down. Yesterday is history, tomorrow is a mystery, today is a gift—that is why they call it the present!

ATTITUDE

Gallup surveyed more than 100,000 employees in a number of different industries finding that when employees held a majority of the following "attitudes," worker satisfaction and company productivity were higher. The employee attitudes identified were:

1. I know what is expected of me at work.
2. I have the materials and equipment I need to do my work.
3. At work, I have the opportunity to do what I do best every day.
4. In the past seven days, I have received recognition or praise for doing good work.
5. My supervisor or someone at work seems to care about me as a person.
6. Someone at work encourages my development.
7. In the past six months, someone at work has talked to me about my progress.
8. At work, my opinions seem to count.
9. The mission/purpose of my company makes me feel my job is important.
10. My fellow employees are committed to doing quality work.
11. I have a best friend at work.
12. This past year, I have had opportunities at work to learn and grow.

It Starts in the Mind

Did you hear about the frog who was hopping along one day, when he happened to slip into a large pothole? All his attempts to jump out fell short. Soon a cat came upon the frog trapped in the hole and offered to pull him out. He too failed. Several other animals tried to help the poor frog, but they all gave up. "We'll go back and get you some food," they said. "It looks like you're going to be there a while." However, not long after they took off to get food, the frog hopped past them. They couldn't believe it! "We thought you couldn't get out of there," they hollered. "Oh, I couldn't," replied the frog, "but you see, there was a big tractor coming right at me and I had to." That's how it is with many people. Only when they *have* to get out of potholes and the ruts of life do they make changes.

Time to Kick it Up a Notch

So many people in this world have many more problems and challenges than you and I face daily. Whether it's physical, emotional, or any other type of problem, they still succeed and prosper. Why? Because they have come to understand that the only barrier between them and anything they desire is the way they think. They understand that their life today is the way it is because of what's been programmed into their mind, which produces how they think. So we need to change the way we think and reprogram our minds. This is where the right attitudes are birthed.

Let's take a look at how the mind works. Your mind is the control mechanism of your entire life. Once we begin to understand what is going on in our mind, we can see how our thoughts operate, and we begin to realize that any and all of our goals and dreams are possible. Your mind is a magnificent tool and when you know how to use it, it will be a powerful tool to help you become what you want to be. After all, you can't control what happens to you, but you can control your attitude toward what happens to you. It all begins in the mind.

CURIOSITY

I recently had the privilege of meeting and breaking bread with the legendary basketball Coach John Wooden. At 94, not only is he one of the most humble and genuine people I have ever met, but he also gave me a nugget of wisdom I want to share with you. He said, "Always remember, adversity will make you stronger if you learn from it." Think about the greatest lessons you have learned in life. They most likely came in the midst of crisis or adversity. We have to continue to be lifetime students. Let's continue to learn and extract the lessons from everything that comes our way (both the positive and negative). And for those of you who already know everything, remember coach Wooden's other famous quote, "It is what you learn after you know it all that counts."

Be and Stay Curious

It was Samuel Johnson who once said, "Curiosity is, in great and generous minds, the first passion and the last." With that thought in mind, always remember in both your professional and personal life to make sure you're constantly asking questions. Cultivate your curiosity. Prepare your questions and don't ever be too busy to listen. Most of us do the opposite. We prepare our answers. We rehearse what we are going to say. We polish our presentations, not realizing that our clients would rather talk than listen to us.

In business, we all know that when a prospective customer decides to sign a contract, they want to do business with someone who is interested in them. They want someone who understands them and who will be a good consultant to them. To show a prospect or anyone else that you are interested, you must be the person who asks the most thoughtful questions. To convince a company that you're the best choice over the competition, you will have to out-learn them by your creativity and quantity of your questions. Great relationship builders ultimately learn that the sale most often goes to the most interested party, and that your level of interest will be measured by the quantity and quality of your questions. You might be thinking that this might not apply to you because you're not in business or don't sell for a living, but always remember the words of Robert Louis Stevenson, "Everybody lives by selling something." Stay curious and keep asking questions. School may be out but your education never ends!

Three Great Thoughts on Curiosity:

"One of the secrets of life is to keep our intellectual curiosity acute."
—William Phelps

"Seize the moment of excited curiosity on any subject to solve your doubt. For if you let it pass, the desire may never return and you may remain in ignorance."
—Unknown

"Life must be lived and curiosity kept alive. One must never, for whatever reason, turn his back on his life."
—Eleanor Roosevelt

COURAGE

Courage is much more than a feeling. Check the record—anybody who ever beat the odds did it in spite of their fear! They did it because they were inspired by somebody else's example or words, they were moved by a need, and they said to themselves, "If not me, who? If not now, when?" They didn't think much about it at all or they might have changed their mind. If you are waiting for a feeling of courage, forget about it because it doesn't exist! You're only courageous when you do what's right—despite your fear. And since all of us feel fear, every one of us is capable of acting courageously. It's a choice! Whatever you do, you need courage. It can be moral courage, the courage of your convictions or the courage to see things through. Any time you go where you've never been or try something you've never done, fear will be present. It will always stand between you and anything worth doing. Courage is overcoming and mastering fear—not the absence of fear. The choice is yours!

Wisdom for Leaders

Why do some executives get fired while others grow and flourish? The American Management Association conducted in-depth interviews with 41 top executives and found that these traits often lead to failure (in no particular order):

1. Insensitivity to co-workers
2. Aloofness and arrogance
3. Tendency to misuse information conveyed in confidence
4. Inability to control ambition
5. Inability to delegate assignments
6. Inability to staff effectively
7. Inability to think strategically
8. Overdependence on mentors

Remember, to lead people you can't just have knowledge but need wisdom to make prudent and effective decisions.

Leading and Teaching Others

A study conducted by the U.S. Department of Health, Education and Welfare reported the following:

Learners retain:
10% of what they read
20% of what they hear
30% of what they see
50% of what they see and hear
70% of what they SAY
80% of what they SAY and DO

The lesson is a very simple one, yet often ignored. It is not enough to know. (How many times have you coached or advised someone and they say, "I know, I know?") You must say it and then do it!

"The positive thinker sees the difficulty in every opportunity;
an optimist sees the opportunity in every difficulty."
—Winston Churchill

THOUGHTS

We have all heard the old adage, "You are what you think," but the truth is, your thought condition will influence your life condition. Many people hurt their chance for success by sabotaging themselves with negative thought patterns, not understanding that those thought patterns will ultimately influence their behavior. One of the major influences of your thought condition is the people surrounding you. Negative thinkers tend to surround themselves with negative and discouraging people. They feel comfortable in these surroundings, because they don't have to live up to anyone's expectations, and, therefore, they have an excuse to fail. These people are dangerous, because their views are contagious and erode self-esteem. Do you surround yourself with people who believe in you and lift your spirits? Or do you spend time with people who bring you down? Surround yourself with positive thoughts and positive people every day!

Enough Talk

One of the most insidious obstacles to taking action is procrastination. If you are waiting for everything to be perfect (just right) before you take action, you never will. The people who use this excuse confuse the word "hard" with the word "impossible." It is not impossible to change jobs—just hard. It is not impossible to lose weight—just hard. It is not impossible to move to another city—just hard. The tendency to see "hard" as "impossible" is closely tied to resisting change. Do not allow yourself to believe that because something is hard, it is impossible. Most things are possible, if you believe and take action.

The time to make sales calls is today. The time to start working out is today. The time to start working on a project is today. And the time to start picking up the pieces and begin over again is today! The best day to begin anything is today, so get started. No matter what your problems are and no matter how long you have procrastinated, get started today!

Your Work and Your Life

OUR WORK
Do your work.
Not just your work and no more,
But a little more for the lavishing sake.
That little more which is worth
All the rest.

And when you suffer as you must,
And if you sometimes doubt, as you will—do your work.
Put your heart into it.
Give it your best.
The sky will one day clear.

Then, out of your very doubt
And suffering will be born
The supreme joy that comes from work well done.

—*Dean Briggs, Northwestern University*

Give your work and give your life everything you've got!

> "Wealth, notoriety, place and power are no measures of success whatsoever. The only true measure of success is the ratio between what we might have been and what we have become."
>
> —H.G. Wells

SUCCESS

D o you link success to money, power or fame? In 1828, Noah Webster wrote the first dictionary, and he used these four words to define success: Fortunate, prosperous, happy and contentment. Three of the four adjectives he used to define success had nothing to do with money. And there lies the great dilemma in America today. You like the things money can buy—it can buy you a nice car, suit, house or boat. But you *love* the things it can't buy. It can't buy you peace, health, love, character, integrity, tenacity, perseverance or enthusiasm. Success is reaching your maximum potential by being committed to excellence in everything you do. Remember, success should always be linked to excellence and fulfillment!

You Want Success? You Gotta Work!

No matter where I go, everyone I meet wants to be successful. Success...everyone wants it, but what exactly is success, and how do you attain it?

When I was 13 years old, my mother came home from work and brought me a wooden box that would forever change my life. On the outside of the box were the words "The secret of success." When I opened the little wooden box, I saw the four letter word, "WORK."

That was the day I began to understand more about success. I learned that if you want to be successful, you are going to have to work. There is no quick fix, magic wand, potion or short cut to help you attain the levels of success you have always dreamed of.

So how do you become successful?

Here are four keys you must remember on your success journey:

1. **Focus and concentrate on one main goal.** You can do almost anything, but you cannot do everything!If you are going to succeed in this life, you are going to have to unclutter your life, get rid of distractions and **focus!**Focus on your goal, focus on continual improvement and focus on the future.

2. **Sacrifice.** Once you decide where to focus your attention and energy, you must decide what you are willing to give up to attain it. There are thousands of people who want to earn more money, but they do not want to work harder. They want success, but they are not willing to pay the price. Are you willing to pay the price to have success in your career? Your marriage? Your spiritual life? Financial life? Your health? There is no success without sacrifice.

3. **Forget the past and focus on the future.** Maybe you have made mistakes in your life (we all have) or you have had a difficult past (we all have). Work your way through it and move on. There are only two types of people in this world: those who have been hurt and those who have been hurt more. What happens in life happens to all of us. If you do not bury your past, it will bury your future.

4. **The secret of your success is found in your daily decisions and routine.** What you do today determines success tomorrow. If you plan and prepare for the future (your family, your friends, career, health, priorities, etc.), it's just a matter of time before you begin to experience and see the manifestations of your dreams.

PATIENCE

Some of your greatest mistakes will happen because of impatience. Patience is not just the ability to wait; it's the ability to keep a good attitude while you're waiting. In 1879, a man called Pearl Wait invented Jell-O. He tried selling it door-to-door with other homemade remedies that he had invented, but when sales weren't strong, he sold his rights for $450 to a man called Woodward. Woodward knew the value of marketing and long-term planning, and within eight years, he had turned Jell-O into a million-dollar business. Today, not one of Pearl Wait's relatives receives a penny in royalties from the 1.1 million boxes of Jell-O that are sold daily. Why? Because Pearl Wait couldn't wait! Life is a marathon, not a 50-yard dash. Learn to pace yourself!

There's No Room for Chips

There is an old expression that says, "When you carry responsibility on your shoulders, there is no room for chips." Many people in our society want to blame their problems on their past, their spouse, their race, the government, their employer, their children, their employees, their customers, the economy, and anything or anyone else they can find to blame. You hear it from 5-year-olds to politicians. Collectively as a society, we are suffering from what *U.S. News & World Report* called "it's-not-my-fault syndrome." Everyone has an excuse and, rarely does anyone want to accept blame. The person most responsible for your success can be found every morning at 7 a.m. or earlier, gazing lovingly into the bathroom mirror. That is the person who must be on a constant journey of improvement. You must recognize that you are in control and that life is somewhat like a game in which you are on the playing field every minute of the day. You are the player and coach all in one.

In this game, you have control of the here and now, no control of the past, and just a little control of the future. All based on your own decisions and actions. The power to fulfill your dreams is within you. You alone have the responsibility to shape and define your life. You are the only person responsible for pushing yourself forward or holding yourself back. The power to succeed or fail is yours alone.

How do I know this to be a fact? Besides reading the biographies of the most successful people in the history of our country and studying some of the current high achievers in the areas of business, politics and athletics, I have experienced the power of taking personal responsibility firsthand.

I am a Hispanic male, grew up in a single parent home and didn't have a wealthy family (my mother raised three of us on her small salary), so the odds were already against me. As if that weren't enough, in my early years, I had a stuttering problem. I started working at age 11 cutting grass. When I graduated from high school, I had to borrow some money and work full-time to put myself through college. When I graduated from college, I had a full-time job as a salesman for a business newspaper. The rest, as they say, is history.

I overcame a speech impediment and financial obstacles to complete my college education. I have no doubt that you can overcome any challenges you're facing today and probably will do better!It simply is a question of whether you are willing to take personal responsibility and live your life in accordance with the old axiom, "If it is to be, it is up to me!" You are the only one who has to live your life. Most people can relate to a sign I once read that said, "If you could kick the person responsible for most of your troubles, you wouldn't be able to sit down for weeks."

> "You can turn painful situations around through laughter.
> If you can find humor in anything, you can survive it."
> —Bill Cosby

STRESS

W hen was the last time you woke up refreshed, refueled and ready for the day? How long did you stay energized and excited about the day's activities? For too many people, the stress of life zaps their ability to do their best, be their best and enjoy their daily activities. More than 1 million Americans have heart attacks each year; 8 million have stomach ulcers. We have more than 12 million alcoholics in this country. These are just the tip of the iceberg of stress-related statistics. Stress is the wear and tear on your body caused by life's events. It's the body's physical, mental and chemical reactions to circumstances in your life. Most people take better care of their cars than they do of themselves. Learn to relax; it's cheaper than therapy. Take a recess; exercise, which will rejuvenate your system; and recognize your limits. If you adapt and create good habits you'll be on your way toward a healthy lifestyle.

Keeping the Right Perspective

I once heard a man say, "We don't stop laughing because we grow old; we grow old because we stop laughing." How true! It's time for a laugh. A variety of studies have shown that laughter is good medicine and that more companies are taking notice. If you're looking to boost productivity, relieve stress, lower your blood pressure and think more clearly, it is time to start laughing more. In fact, it has been reported that 96% of U.S. executives surveyed believe that employees that maintain a sense of humor while working actually work better than their humorless peers. A study at California State University, Long Beach, discovered that people who have fun at work get along better with their co-workers and are more productive and creative then other employees. They also discovered that these employees are more punctual and use fewer sick days. I think too many of us have become far too serious. Smiles, chuckles and good ol' belly laughs have been replaced with flat expressions, stomach aches and ulcers. As Erma Bombeck once said, "We sing, 'make a joyful noise unto the Lord' while our faces reflect the sadness of one who just buried a rich

MENTAL SNACKS

aunt who left everything to her pregnant hamster." It's better to laugh at life than to lament over it. Let's learn to loosen up and have fun!

Communicating and Having Fun

Communication is serious business. Yet, one can't help but laugh at some comical results our communication efforts sometimes produce. Here are a few I have collected over the years:

"The events in our household this past week have left me in a state of consternation," lamented Mrs. Smith. Her friend quickly advised, "Why don't you try prune juice?"

Sportscaster Buddy Diliberto on television announcing the retirement of Hall of Fame Football quarterback Dan Fouts, "After harassing secretaries for 16 years, Dan Fouts is retiring from football." Secretaries should have been secondaries!

She: "Before we got married, you told me you were well off."
He: "I was and I didn't know it."

Wife: "Is it true that money talks?"
Husband: "That's what they say."
Wife: "Well, leave a little here to talk to me today. I get so lonely."

"Things are more like they are now than they have ever been."
—*Former President Gerald Ford*

"Faith is to believe what we do not see; and the reward of this faith is to see what we believe."

—St. Augustine

CHANGE

In 1100 A.D., the following words were inscribed on the tomb of an English bishop in Westminster: "In my youth, my imagination had no limits. I dreamed of changing the world. But as I grew older and wiser, I found that the world would not change, so I decided to change my country. But it, too, seemed immovable. So as I grew into my twilight years, in one last attempt, I settled for changing my family, but they would have none of it. Now on my death bed, I realize that if only I had first changed *myself*, then by example, I might have changed my family, and through my family changed my country, and through my country changed the world." Novelist Leo Tolstoy once said, "Everyone thinks of changing the world, but no one thinks of changing themselves." Any change you desire should begin with you. In order to change your world, you must change yourself!

Warning to the Wise

Leon Martel, in *Mastering Change, the Key To Business Success*, describes three common traps that keep most of us from recognizing and leveraging change:

1. Believing that yesterday's solutions will solve today's problems.

2. Assuming present trends will continue.

3. Neglecting the opportunities offered by future change.

The lesson is a simple one. Don't get caught in the trap of believing that old ideas will succeed in the future.

More on Change

A Canadian neurosurgeon discovered some dramatic truths about the human mind's reaction to change. He conducted various experiments, which proved that when a person is forced to change a fundamental belief or opinion, the brain undergoes a series of nervous sensations equivalent to distressing torture.

Change is not something to be feared but to be embraced. Change is something we should welcome, because without change, nothing in this world would ever grow or blossom, nor would anyone move forward to become the person they want to be or achieve their goals.

In the final analysis, the toughest thing to change is our approach to change. Maybe it's time for a mind transformation that welcomes the advent of change. Expect change, baby, because it is inevitable!

The Process of Changing

There is a great Chinese Proverb that says, "Be not afraid of growing slowly, be only afraid of standing still." In other words, if you are not changing or constantly being transformed, you're in trouble. Personal transformation means the process of changing. It also means to metamorphose, to reconstruct, to modify and to make over. Every person on the planet has to be on the constant journey of growth and change. The alternative is being staid, which means to be sedate, settled, resisting change and stuck in the comfort zone.

Today I want to challenge you not to be complacent or satisfied with your life. Understand that every one of us can be better as a spouse, parent, leader or employee. You can get to another level spiritually, physically and mentally. One of the greatest gifts you can ever give yourself is to make a commitment to become a lifetime student in the classroom of change. To the fearful, change is threatening because they worry things won't go right or may get worse. But to those who dream and aspire for more in life, change is a stimulus! Remember, one change makes way for the next, giving us the opportunity to grow. Hey, it's *your* life and it's *your* choice!

> "Real excellence doesn't come cheaply. A certain price
> must be paid in terms of practice, patience and persistence."
> —Stephen Covey

EXCELLENCE

An elderly carpenter was ready to retire, so he told his employer of his plans to leave the house-building business. The contractor was sorry to see one of the best workers go and asked if he could build one more house as a favor. The carpenter agreed, but it was easy to see that his heart was not in his work. He cut corners and used inferior materials. It was an unfortunate way to end his career. When the house was finished, the contractor came to inspect it and handed the front door key to the carpenter. "This is my gift to you," he said. "It is your house." What a shock! What a shame! If only the carpenter had known he was building his own house, he would have done it all so differently. Remember that you are the carpenter of your life. Each day you hammer a nail, place a board or erect a wall. Build wisely. It is the only life you will ever build! Give it your best.

Everything Should Start with a Commitment to Excellence

We talk about it, think about it, write about it and even contemplate about trying to achieve it. But what is excellence? Charles Dickens' David Copperfield once said, "Whatever I have tried to do in my life, I have tried with all my heart to do well. What I have devoted myself to, I have devoted myself to completely." A.W. Tozer provided a possible definition when he said, "Let your heart soar as high as it will. Refuse to be average."

However you define excellence, it is important to understand that it is not a project, act or job description; excellence is a way of life. It includes going beyond the normal call of duty, stretching our perceived limits and holding ourselves responsible for doing and being our best. Excellence comes from striving, maintaining the highest standards, paying attention to little details and being willing to go the extra mile. Have you made a commitment to excellence? Would others describe your work or your way of life as excellent? Never settle for good enough.

On a closing note, when you think you've arrived at excellence and can now relax...beware. Don't be like the master window washer who, upon doing a superb job with the windows on the 116th floor of the Empire State building, made the mistake of stepping back to admire her work.

Remember, striving for excellence is what keeps the customers coming back!

Developing and Keeping an Edge

It's time to take inventory. Everyone I meet is looking for an edge in his or her field. We have to first take inventory of ourselves. What worked for you and what didn't work for you throughout this past year? What can you do better next year? Here are six ideas that will give you the edge you're looking for:

1. Show that you care by your attitude, your words and action!
2. Deliver *more* than your customers, friends and family expect.
3. Treat customers not the way you want to be treated, but the way they want to be treated—like gold!
4. Plan all your work and work your plan.
5. Knock out today's jobs *today*...not tomorrow. Be known as a finisher.
6. Make right your first impression and all impressions.

THE MIND

Every problem is a mind problem. So many people in the world have many more problems and challenges than you do today, yet they still succeed and prosper, whether their problems are physical or emotional. Why? Because they have come to understand that the only barrier between them and anything they desire is the way they think. Your mind is the control mechanism of your entire life. It is a magnificent tool, and when you know how to use it, it will be a powerful tool to help you become and accomplish what you want. For instance, when you misspell a word on paper, where does the error come from—from the pencil, your hand, your fingers or the paper? None of these. The error comes from your mind. In the same way, a rewarding career, fulfilling relationships, wisdom, good health and wealth all begin in your mind before they manifest in your outer world. When you change your way of thinking, you will change your life forever!

Transforming Your Mind

It was the apostle Paul who said, "Do not be conformed to this world but be transformed by the renewing of your mind." I believe he was saying, don't allow the negativity and cynicism of this world to take permanent residency in your mind.

On a daily basis, make sure you're feeding your mind doses of educational material that can help you grow, spiritual information that will refresh your soul, positive data that will help you be solution-oriented and keep all things in the right perspective. In case you haven't noticed, we live in a negative world. I believe 80% of the world functions from a negative perspective. If you don't' believe me, just watch the news or read the headlines in your daily paper. If that is all you do, very rarely will you be inspired and positive about the future.

What are you reading on a daily basis to assure your growth? What are you allowing your eyes to see and ears to hear? Beware because your eyes and ears are the gateway to your mind. Everything starts in the mind. An ancient proverb says, "As a man or woman thinketh, so he or she is." Happiness and success begin between your ears. Your mind is the drawing table for tomorrow's circumstances. Make sure you guard it!

We Need Wisdom

Wisdom comes from the experience of living. To travel the road of wisdom requires knowledge of our God, others and ourselves. To experience life and learn its truth—this is wisdom. It was Samuel Smiles who said, "Practical wisdom is only to be learned in the school of experience. Precepts and instructions are useful so far as they go, but, without the discipline of real life, they remain of the nature of theory only."

The Book of Proverbs in the Bible is one of my all-time favorites. It is one that I read almost on a daily basis. Its excellent principles for guiding one's life come to us in the form of poetry with clear instructions, principles, values and intellect to succeed in life. Here are some quick lessons in leadership from Proverbs:

1. Good leadership begins with wisdom and insight.
2. Competency cannot make up for lack of character.
3. Leaders who solve problems will never lack followers.
4. Wisdom is available to all who pursue it diligently, but it is not automatic.
5. Rewards always await those who do the right things.
6. Wise leaders not only give good advice; they heed it.

"Commitment is what transforms a promise into reality."
—James Womack

LEGACIES

Years ago, a sociological study asked 50 people over the age of 95 this question: "If you could live your life over again, what would you do differently?" It was an open-ended question with several responses. However, three answers constantly emerged and dominated the results of the study: 1) If I had it to do over again, I would *reflect* more, 2) If I had it to do over again, I would *risk* more, and 3) If I had it to do over again, I would do more things that would live on after I've died. Every day you have a chance to make a positive impact on your co-workers and customers. You can leave a heritage to your children that will last them a lifetime. You can leave a legacy in your company, industry and community. Make a commitment today. Make your life count!

The Radical Leap

There is a good little book out titled, *The Radical Leap,* by Steve Farber. Farber reminds all of us that commitment is one of the key ingredients to succeeding and impacting our world. Here it is:

"Without the calling and commitment of your heart, there's no good reason for you to take a stand, to take risk, to do what it takes to change your world for the better."

Very seldom can you keep a committed person from success. Place a stumbling block in their way, and they create stepping stones to climb to greatness. The people who win in life have plans and execute them. They don't give up every time an obstacle gets in their way. If they can't go over them, they will go through them. In the end, commitment is what gives us power to get through any adversity that comes our way. What are you committed to? Who are you committed to? Remember, decisions are made with your head, but commitments are made with your heart!

The Chicken and the Pig

Many times people think they are committed but aren't. It's like the time a chicken and a pig were talking about commitment. The chicken said, "I'm committed to giving eggs every morning." The pig said, "Giving eggs isn't commitment, it's participation. Giving ham is total commitment!"

Make Every Minute Count

The great Benjamin Franklin once said, "If we take care of the minutes, the years will take care of themselves." One minute. It doesn't seem like much. However, if you were to place a one-dollar value on every minute of your life, in *one year*, you would have $525,600. Are you spending or investing your minutes? Time is a fixed income, and as with any income, the real challenge facing you is how to work successfully with your daily allotment. Plan each day down to the minute, because once you have wasted time, you can never get it back. The value you place on each minute of every day will determine the results you get in your life. Don't count the minutes, but make every minute count!

> "If you aren't fired up with enthusiasm,
> then you will be fired with enthusiasm!"
> —Vince Lombardi

ENTHUSIASM

Enthusiasm is an essential element if you are to have success. Enthusiasm is a zeal; it is fire and passion inside you. Enthusiasm separates those who just *want* to be successful from those who *are* successful. It will transform your life, because it produces energy. If you are excited about something, you are more likely to work harder to attain it. Enthusiasm is like adrenaline, pushing you to accomplish more with greater efficiency. Enthusiasm takes commitment, and commitment takes work. You are not going to get out of bed fired up every day, but it is up to you to change your attitude to a positive one. After all, what use is negative energy? It drains you of your most precious resource—your enthusiasm.

Enthusiasm Makes the Difference

Years ago Norman Vincent Peale wrote a book entitled, *Enthusiasm Makes the Difference.* In it, he detailed a formula that may help you put every day in a positive, uplifting prospective.

1. The first step is to, "Think a good day." If you have a positive image of the day before it unfolds, it will help get you going in the right direction.
2. The second step is to, "Thank a good day." Give thanks for a good day in advance and that positive imagery helps make it so.
3. Thirdly, "Plan a good day." Put some positive things into your day to help get it on the right track and keep it there.
4. Next, "Put good into the day." Put good thoughts, good attitudes and good actions into a day and they will make the day good.
5. Finally, "Fill the day with enthusiasm." Give the day all you've got and it will give it right back to you. Enthusiasm can make a difference in a day, a job and in your life.

Think a good day and you will have one.

Enthusiasm Is a Way of Life

Remember, enthusiasm isn't something you "put on" and "take off" to fit an occasion. Enthusiasm is a way of life. Find something that excites you and consumes you, something that is worthy to build your life around. You will only have significant success with something you have enthusiasm for!

Enthusiasm fuels your dream. Anything that you neglect will deteriorate. It could be your body, your marriage or the dream of your life. Enthusiasm will give you and those around you the energy, drive and encouragement to stay focused. What are you dreaming about today? What do you long to finish or achieve? Here are three keys to help you release the power of enthusiasm around you:

1. Create a visual representation or written goal and place it on the wall so you can look at it every day. Before and while I wrote my first book, I looked at the title every day.
2. Find people who believe in you and your dreams, people who will encourage and support you.
3. Realize that you are responsible for maintaining your own enthusiasm and the energy for achieving your dreams. It's not the responsibility of your spouse or boss. Remind yourself to take daily steps to create the climate of continuous victory in your life!

"The most important thing in communication
is to hear what isn't being said."
—Peter Drucker

COMMUNICATION

The words you use on a daily basis often determine the success and failure of your interactions with your spouse, co-workers or clients. According to research psychologists, the average one-year-old child has a three-word vocabulary. By 15 months of age, children can speak 19 words. At two years of age, most youngsters possess a working knowledge of 272 words. Their vocabulary catapults to 896 words by the age of three, 1,540 by age four and 2,072 words by age five. By age six, the average child can communicate with 2,562 words. Our word accumulation continues to grow, yet using the words effectively does not necessarily follow. When communicating, say what you mean and mean what you say!

The word "communication" comes from the Latin root "commune," which means "held in common." To make communication work, we have to make sure that the people we're talking with understand what we're saying as well as we do. Think about this scenario:

A construction worker approached the reception desk in a doctor's office. The receptionist asked him why he was there. "I have shingles," he said. She took his name, address, medical insurance number and told him to have a seat. Twenty-five minutes later he was called into a room, and when the doctor arrived, he asked him what he had. The man said, "shingles." The doctor said, "Where?" He said, "Outside in the truck. Where do you want them?"

The lesson is a simple one: Make sure people understand exactly what you're trying to say. Communication is not just about sending a message but also about shared meaning and understanding.

The Power of Words

Words are powerful. Choose them carefully. Before you speak, organize not only your thoughts, but determine which words best communicate the message you want to send. If you're going to be effective, you have to attempt to speak in the other person's language rather than your own. Mark Twain put it this way: "The difference between using the right words and the almost right words is the difference between lightning and the lightning bug." Remember, words stir emotions, cause wars, close sales, mend relationships, kill deals, strengthen or weaken marriages and can bring you closer or further away from your dreams.

One Last Thought on Communication

Remember, silence has never been misquoted. Make sure you don't just speak to hear yourself. Many people have regretted their speech but never their silence.

> "All your strength is in union, all your danger is in discord."
> —Unknown

TEAMWORK

S omeone once said, "Coming together is a beginning; keeping together is progress; working together is success." They were right. One day a father called his six sons together to teach them a lesson that would help them throughout their life. He had already gathered a bundle of six sticks, which he had carefully tied together with a string. One by one, he asked his six sons to take the bundle and break it. All six of them failed. Then the father took out a knife and cut the string and distributed a single stick to each of the six sons. He repeated the request that they break the single stick. This time, each son broke his stick. The father looked at them and said, "When you work together in a spirit of harmony, you resemble the bundle of sticks, and no one can defeat you, but when you quarrel among yourselves, anyone can defeat you one at a time." Remember, a house or team divided against itself cannot stand or win!

A Team Has One Heart

A solid team will always have many voices but only one heart. One of the keys to building a successful team is to effectively communicate with each other. Besides being committed to the vision and competency for the job you've got to have a strategy to make sure teammates stay connected to each other and have accessibility with one another. To enhance your effectiveness in communicating, remember these keys:

1. **Follow up your communication in writing.** The larger the team, staff or organization, the more difficult it becomes to communicate. That is why you should follow up by communicating in writing. Football teams have playbooks, businesses have employee manuals, marriages have vows and partnerships have contracts because it easier to keep everyone on the same page.

2. **Be candid.** This was a struggle for me early in my career because I didn't want to hurt anyone's feelings. Then you learn that you do people a disservice by not telling them the truth up front. Open com-

MENTAL SNACKS

munication fosters trust. Sugarcoating bad news and communicating via a third party hurts relationships. The goal is to always speak with truth and firmness, but also with kindness, to your teammates.

3. **Be inclusive.** When and if you can include everyone with information, do so. Obviously, there is some sensitive information you need to be discreet with, but remember that open communication increases trust and trust increases ownership. When people are in the loop they feel connected to the organization.

Remember, no employer, regardless of their industry or trade is independent of those around them. You can't succeed alone, no matter how great your ability or amount of capital you have. Successful businesses and winning teams today are about cooperation and communication with each other.

CHALLENGES

No matter who you are, "challenges" are just part of life. Think about this for a moment: the salesman has his quotas; the performer has his rehearsals; the pilot has to stay strapped in for hours; the minister is never free from sermon preparation. How about the truck driver who deals with the daily grind of traffic, weather hazards and monotonous miles? Then there's the mother with tiny children, facing 14 hours a day of making decisions, competing with strong wills and trying to be everything to everybody. Everyone has been given an assignment that comes with a challenge. The poet said, "I grumbled that I had no shoes, till I met a man who had no feet." It's all about attitude. And with the right perspective and attitude you can overcome any challenge in your life.

We've Got to Overcome

Thomas Edison said, "Many of life's failures are men who did not realize how close they were to success when they gave up."

The truth is, all successful people fail, but they keep trying. Thomas Edison did. So can you. Evaluate your life today. If you are not as successful as you want to be, maybe it is because you have not failed enough. The defining difference between successful people and unsuccessful people is not intelligence level, family background or whom they know. It is perseverance!

Success, winning, victory and riches go to the individual who is willing to persevere. Perseverance is the power to hold on in spite of everything. To endure and face defeat without giving up is the power of perseverance. People who are successful never quit because their perseverance won't let them. They realize that failure is merely a temporary setback to their goal or dream. Many will tell them it can't be done, but they don't listen, because they keep their eyes focused on their goals. They don't let failure distract them. Always remember, getting knocked down is not a disgrace—staying down is.

Challenges Are Part of Life

In order to overcome any challenges, you're going to have to understand the importance of persistence and perseverance. So, how do you know when you have persevered enough? When you achieve what you set out to do, then it's enough. Think about these examples:

- Michelangelo endured seven years lying on his back on a scaffold to paint the Sistine Chapel.
- Michael Jordan was cut from his high school basketball team.
- Vince Lombardi didn't become a head coach in the NFL until he was 47.
- In his first three years in the automobile business, Henry Ford went bankrupt twice.
- Dr. Seuss' first children's book was rejected by 23 publishers. The 24th publisher sold 6 million copies.
- During its first year in business, the Coca-Cola Company sold only 400 Cokes.

The lesson—Don't quit, don't stop and don't ever give up!

NEW BEGINNINGS

The beginning of a new year is always a time of the year that people begin to think about New Year resolutions. Approximately 100 million Americans will enthusiastically usher in the New Year with several resolutions in mind. According to a study by the University of Washington, "increasing the amount of exercise" was the most common primary resolution, being made by 37% of subjects. It was followed by "increased time devoted to work or study," 23%, and "increasing the consumption of healthy food or decreasing the amount of unhealthy food," 13%. What are your goals? What New Year resolutions do you have in mind?

It is one thing to make a resolution, and it's another thing to see that resolution become a reality. Various studies and research conclude that in order to successfully achieve your resolutions or goals you must do the following three things:

1. Make a firm commitment.
   (That means writing them down on paper.)

2. Have a strategy to accomplish your goals.

3. Keep track of your progress, celebrating victories along the way.

How many goals have you set? How powerful are your plans and desires to achieve them? What price are you willing to pay to make them come true? Your answers will determine whether you want to be a spectator or an active participant in the game of life.

Goals Determine Your Future

The first reason you need to have goals is that they will give you power and drive in your life. The second reason is that your future does not get better by just hoping. Your future gets better by planning. You need to have goals before you can begin planning your future!

Most people just think of goals in terms of their work or their weight. This is a good beginning, but don't stop there. You need to have goals for the other facets of your life. For example, your marriage, your family, your spiritual life, your relationships, your intellectual life (continuing education) and financial life are all important areas we need to consider as we set our goals for the New Year. I personally break mine down into three categories:

1. **Personal Goals**—these deal with my family, health, marriage, home, etc.

2. **Professional Goals**—these deal with work-related issues, accounts, projects, budgets, new initiatives, etc.

3. **Self-Developmental Goals**—these deal with how I am going to improve my quality of life by growing spiritually, intellectually and physically.

The point is not so much how you do your goals but that you have them and write them down. So get excited about your future and aim high!

"If you want to be somebody, if you want to go somewhere,
you better wake up and pay attention!"

—Sister Act 2

WORDS

Your tongue is one of the most powerful gifts ever placed at your command. Life and death are in the power of the tongue. So often we do not think before we speak or consider the effect our words will have. Words like "I can't do that," "I can't handle it" or "This will never change" don't just affect those around you—they also infect *you*! Words have power because they create your world. More than anything that anyone else says, you believe what comes out of your own mouth. Refuse to release words of defeat, depression and discouragement. Your words are life! By thinking and speaking positively, you open the doors to make your optimism come true. Your words have the ability to build or destroy. Make sure you use them wisely!

Think and Speak

It has been said that we will live one-fifth of our lives speaking. Yet I am amazed every day at the number of people who waste and spend their words so cheaply.

As you know, words are powerful. Make sure you think before you speak. I say the word "think" because many don't, and because you can use "T-H-I-N-K" as an acronym to make sure your words are productive and powerful. Think about this:

Truthful—If you always tell the truth you will never have to remember what you said.

Helpful—To the proportion that you help other people either by teaching, training, coaching, or correcting, they will help you.

Informative—The value of the knowledge you share or education you give is determined by its ability to help others grow.

Necessary—Silence cannot be misquoted. Never discuss your problems with someone who can't solve them. Know when to talk and when to listen.

Kind—Life is too short. Be silent instead of discussing the shortcomings or weaknesses of others. If what you say to someone can't be said to everyone, then say it to no one.

Learn More Words

Not only is it important to choose your words carefully, but you must have an array of words to choose from in your vocabulary. The English language has more than 450,000 words. Most of our daily conversations are made up of a mere 400 words. That means we only use .0008% of words available to us, and, unfortunately, some of the most common used are I, me and my. While going to college full time and working full time at a business newspaper, I started reading and listening to material that reinforced the fact that there is a direct correlation between the number of words you use in your vocabulary and the amount of money you will make in your career. Research by management and human resources experts have confirmed that no matter what the field of employment, people with large vocabularies (those able to speak clearly, using simple and descriptive words) are the most likely to accomplish their goals.

Your ability to articulate and orally communicate will determine how far you can go. The more you learn, the more you earn. Well-chosen and carefully selected words can close the sale, enhance relationships, negotiate your raise and help you attain your goals. You only have one chance to make a first impression. Your ability to communicate with other people is vital for your success.

> "The game of business is very much like the game of tennis.
> Those who fail to master the basics of serving well, usually lose."
> —Unknown

SMILES

Of all the things you put on in the morning, a smile is probably the most valuable. Don't just give your employees or associates instructions—smile while you're doing it. If your husband or wife works in a difficult environment, make sure he or she doesn't come home to more of the same. Smiles are like thermostats—they set the temperature and determine the climate around you. Joy is infectious. How people see you determines how they will treat you. Nobody wants to be around somebody who looks like they'll bite your head off at any moment. Learn to smile; it opens doors and hearts. It causes others to relax and to lower their guard. Smiling says, "I'm happy to be with you" to someone you know, and it says, "I'm glad to meet you" to someone you just met. Whether you wear a smile or have a positive attitude, the choice is yours alone!

What Business Are You In?

Have you thought about what business you're in lately? Ask most people, and they'll say things like banking, sales, insurance, software, hospitality, healthcare, advertising, retail, etc. If that were the kind of answer you'd give, you would only be halfway right. If your clients or customers went away for good, what type of business would you be in then? Would you still have a job? Of course not! That means regardless of what industry you're in, you're in the customer service business. In today's marketplace most products and services are becoming a commodity. The only difference in the long-term success of any business will be based on the level of service they deliver and the quality of the relationship. The goal is to become a customer service **ACE**:

Attentive to each customer and their request.
Caring about their needs and problems.
Excited about your services and products.

Think about the very best experience you've had as a customer. What made it so good? Now, think about your worst experience. What made it so bad? Replicate those positive characteristics in your business and eliminate the negative ones in your dealings with customers.

From the Heart

"Customer service doesn't come from a manual, it comes from the heart. When you're taking care of customers, you can never do too much. And there is *no* wrong way, if it comes from the heart."
—*Mrs. Debbie Fields*

Interesting Tidbits

On average...

Satisfied customers tell five people about the good service they received. Dissatisfied customers tell 10 people about the bad service they received.

Of customers who take their business somewhere else:
15% find cheaper products elsewhere.
15% find better products elsewhere.
65% leave because of poor customer service.
—*The Forum Corp.*

"Everyone has an opportunity to be great because
everyone has an opportunity to serve."
—Martin Luther King, Jr.

GIVING

Are you a giver or a taker? Nothing has as much of a positive impact on people as giving to others. People who have a giving spirit are some of the most positive people on earth, because giving is the highest form of living. These people focus their time and energy on what they can give to others rather than what they can get from them. And studies show that the more they give, the better their attitude. Most unsuccessful people don't understand this concept. They think that the amount people give and their attitude are based on how much they have. But that's not true. The fact is, there are plenty of people who have been blessed with money, good families and great careers who are greedy, stingy and suspicious of others. Remember, it's not what you have that makes a difference; it's what you do with what you have. And that is based on your attitude!

It's All about Giving Value

How many people really understand that the more valuable you become, the more the marketplace will reward you? You have to always give value first. Become known as a resource, as a person who gives more than takes. Your value is linked to your knowledge and your willingness to help others. In today's society, knowledge is your passport to success. That's why you have to constantly be on the journey to self-improvement. We live in the information age, yet as a society, people are doing less analytical thinking, disciplined study and reading than ever before. A recent study showed that 50% of Americans do not read books. This is sad because the person who can read and doesn't is no better off than the person who can't read.

Did you know that if you would commit to reading or listening to one nonfiction book per month (that is only 12 a year), you would be in the top 1% in America?

Do you think you would be bringing value to your clients, company and to yourself if you knew more than the competition or your colleague?

One of my mentors taught me that I could make great contributions to my family, community and country if I spent one-third of my life learning, one-third of my life earning and the other one-third of my life serving. I like that concept because life is a gift, and it offers us the opportunity and responsibility to give something back.

TEAMWORK

There is a story about four people, named Everybody, Somebody, Anybody and Nobody. There was an important job to be done and everybody was asked to do it. Everybody was sure somebody would do it, but nobody did it. Somebody got angry about that, because it was everybody's job. Everybody thought anybody could do it, but nobody realized that everybody wouldn't do it. It ended up that everybody blamed somebody when nobody did what anybody could have done. In today's competitive world, too often people either take the entire task upon themselves or they expect that someone else will do their job for them. And in the end, the job never seems to get finished or is never successful because it lacks the winning ingredient called teamwork. A team becomes a champion when everyone labors toward a common goal together.

Working with Other People

The other day I was watching Thomas the Train and his friends with my twin boys. As the trains pulled out of their stations and began to hook up, backup, connect with one another and move to their destination, it occurred to me that it is the same principle we need to apply if we are going to influence others to get the job done. Lessons from watching the trains:

1. To accomplish things—*get on the same track.*
2. To execute—*connect with people.*
3. To complete the mission—*give people a sense of value and direction.*

Too many times we take our co-workers, clients, vendors, family members and others for granted. Asking people politely and thanking them goes a long way in making them feel appreciated (which, by the way, is the No. 1 reason people leave their jobs). Another key is to remember that everybody makes a difference. I remember my first boss and mentor telling me I was the most important person in the company. I was only the courier, but he always made me feel like I was a big part of the team.

Mother Teresa once said, "I can't do what you do and you can't do what I do, but together we can do great things."

Teamwork Requires Checking Your Ego at the Door

Did you know that bees live through the winter by teamwork? They form into a ball and keep up a dance. Then they change places; those that have been out move to the center and those at the center move out. That's how they survive winter. If those at the center insist on staying there, keeping the others at the edges, they would all die. We all need to check our egos at the door and remember to set aside our differences for the good of the team. All great achievements in any great organization are the result of the combined efforts of each individual. No one has ever gotten to the top of their field, whether it is in sports, ministry, politics or business, by themselves. Remember, teamwork will always make the dreamwork.

P.S. A house divided against itself cannot stand!

WORK ON PURPOSE

Do you realize you're not here by accident? You're on this earth on purpose. In my opinion, one of the primary reasons that people get depressed is lack of purpose. Just having the means to live is not enough; a person must have something to live for. If there is no purpose to a person's life then there's no meaning, no reason to get out of bed in the morning. Part of the challenge in life is to understand that a person's real purpose is not just to achieve goals, but to constantly strive toward them. When it comes to our work remember these keys to stay on track:

1. Pursue your *passion* not your pension. Those who only work for money never have any.

2. Make sure you bring *value* to your organization and customers. The more value you bring to the table the more you qualify for promotion and financial rewards.

   Are you solving problems for your boss or creating them?
   Are you serving customers and co-workers with a positive attitude?
   Are you sharing *ideas* and wisdom to help others grow?

3. Working hard on your job can earn you a living but working harder on yourself can earn you a fortune. Are you *learning* and *growing* every day? Do you have a plan for continual growth and education?

The people who ultimately have success in their lives work and live on purpose!

Sacrifice

No matter what you want in life, you are going to have to give up something to get it. Most people are willing to pay $150,000 for a new house, $35,000 for a new car, and $20,000 for a new boat, but very few people are willing to pay the price for success, no matter how much they want it. There is no success without sacrifice. To have a good marriage, to stay in shape or to succeed in business, you will have to sacrifice. You pay a price for everything in life. You pay a price to lose weight. You pay a price to win. You pay a price to get stronger, faster, better. You pay a price for changing, and you even pay a price for staying the same. Can you think of one person in history whose name is worthy of memory who led a life of ease and didn't have to sacrifice anything? What price are you currently paying to attain your goals or dreams? If you are not willing to pay the price for success, you will pay with failure.

Keep It Going

One of my favorite stories is the story of a farmer whose mule fell into the well. Since there was no way to get him out, the farmer decided to bury him there. But the mule had a different idea. Initially, when the shovels of dirt started landing on his back, he became hysterical. Then a thought struck him: "Just shake it off, and step on it." So he did. Hour after hour, as dirt fell on him, he kept telling himself, "Just shake it off, and step on it!" No matter how much dirt the farmer threw at him, he just kept shaking it off and stepping on it, until finally he stepped triumphantly out of the well.

Life will either bury you or bless you; the choice is yours. Storms come for a reason, but they only stay for a season. Extract the lesson and you become wiser. Outlast the storm and you become stronger. Never give up and stay the course!

YOU'VE GOT IT INSIDE

All people are created with the equal ability to become unequal. Not everyone is equipped with the same talents, gifts and abilities; however, each one of us is created in a unique way. Personalities are as diverse as the universe itself. There is one constant: you can, by using what you have to the fullest, stand out from the crowd. Thomas Edison was almost deaf, but he didn't spend his time attempting to learn how to hear. Instead he focused on his ability to think, organize and create. His accomplishments speak well for his decision to build on the qualities he possessed. He took the ability inside of him and made the best of it. Your responsibility is to take the talents and abilities you've been given and develop them to the highest level possible!

Keep Yourself on Track

Many people who have lots of talent and big dreams have lost their drive to achieve them. They have lost the motivation and excitement they once had. When you drive near a cemetery, remember that beneath the soil are many buried dreams, treasures and potential that were never fulfilled because they lost their motivation. You have to fight for your motivation daily. There will be times when you get distracted, your energy dissipates and your dream seems unreachable. But hang on because you *can* and *need* to regain your motivation.

Keys To Motivating Yourself

1. **Stay focused on your goals.** Your focus determines your feelings and your motivation. You were created by God to complete your assignment. Over time you will experience moments of inspiration and surges of enthusiasm over your dreams. However, you will have obstacles and face adversity so you must stay focused. Abraham Lincoln said, "Success is the ability to go from failure to failure without losing your enthusiasm." With all the adversity he experienced he should know.

2. **Make sure you get enough rest.** Fatigue affects your motivation. You can overwork yourself. You need to understand that energy is necessary for success. When fatigue walks in, faith walks out. Tired eyes rarely see a great future. Make sure you're disengaging from time to time and getting good sleep and rest. Refuel your soul and re-energize your batteries consistently.

3. **Get away from unhealthy relationships that drain you.** There are few life-givers but plenty of life-drainers (people who drain you emotionally and mentally). Life-drainers often exist in your own family, friendships and in some colleagues at work. Different relationships exude different levels of energy. Assess your relationships and cut off or limit your exposure to those who leave you empty, exhausted and focused on your problems instead of your future. Life is too short. Pursue those relationships that add to and multiply your life!

> "When faith walks in, fear always leaves."
> —Unknown

OVERCOME YOUR FEARS

The best way of overcoming fear is to take the word *fear* and break it down by its letters, which actually stand for *false evidence appearing real.* When you think of fear in this context, it becomes easier to overcome. Bill Emmerton overcame fear in a big way. Bill, in his late 40s, had set a goal of running through Death Valley. Most people know about the torturing heat, but few know that the valley is 125 miles long. As Bill began his journey, the temperature was 106. He was soon met by a raging sand storm so severe that it picked him up off the ground and blew him 15 feet. But he refused to let fear stop him. Bill kept going. Later, the temperature escalated to 135 degrees and he had to finish with the toe of his shoe cut off to allow for the circulation of blood. Bill didn't let the fear of the heat or desert interfere with his goal—he finished the run. The fear of failure will never overtake you, if you remember that most fears are based on appearances, not reality.

Fight Your Fears and You'll Win

One of your greatest weapons to succeed will be your ability to focus on your primary objectives every day. Focus gives you a distinct vision for your day and your life. However, one of the biggest obstacles in your success journey is fear. Your focus can be destroyed by fear if you allow it. Fear can turn the strong into weak. The powerful into pitiful. To fight fear, you've got to stare it in the face, understand it and overcome it. Don't let fear fool you. Confront the fear, beat it, whip it, defeat it and overcome it by taking the risk and pursuing a new path and opportunity. No risk, no nothing in life!

We will all face opposition. Remember, opposition is often a clue that you're on the right track. Ignore the cynics, naysayers and voices of doom and gloom. They never accomplish anything. As you confront your fears, you will emerge victorious and feel free. Make the decision today to turn your fear into faith, focus and, since we live in America, into fortune!

Winners Conquer Fear

It's pretty simple to tell a winner from a loser. A winner says, "Let's find out;" a loser says, "Nobody knows." When a winner makes a mistake, he says, "I was wrong;" when a loser makes a mistake, he says, "It wasn't my fault." A winner makes commitments; a loser makes only promises. A winner goes through a problem; a loser goes around it, and never gets past it. A winner says, "I'm good, but not as good as I ought to be;" a loser says, "I'm not as bad as a lot of other people." A winner respects those who are superior to him and tries to learn something from them; a loser resents those who are superior to him and tries to find kinks in their armor. A winner feels responsible for more than his job; a loser says, "I only work here." A winner doesn't care who gets the credit; a loser takes all the credit but passes blame. If you want to be a winner, think like a winner, act like a winner, and sooner than you think, you will be a winner!

TIMING AND PREPARATION

Have you heard about the Chinese bamboo tree? During the first four years of its life, it grows only a few inches. Then in the fifth year, it grows 90 feet in just five weeks. Now the real question is, did it grow 90 feet in five weeks or five years? The answer: five years. You see, if at any time during those first four years you'd stopped watering and fertilizing the tree, it would have died. Our lives are like that. They are lived on different levels and arrive in seasons. You stay on one level and learn its lessons until you become qualified to move to the next. Don't be impatient about your goals, dreams or success. We live in a world where many people just want instant money, instant success, instant fame, instant everything! They do not understand timing, preparation and perseverance. It takes time to know your business. It takes time to know your product. It takes time to develop relationships and loyal customers. Don't rush!

Preparation Will Help You Succeed

Many years ago I heard Merlin Olsen say, "One of life's most painful moments comes when we must admit that we didn't do our homework, that we were not prepared when the opportunity came along." He was right. There is a lack of respect for preparation in our world today.

People are looking for instant cash, instant success, instant gratification, instant fame and instant fortune. Not understanding that everything worth value in life takes time to flourish and bloom. We have to be fervent in prayer, fearless in principle, firm in purpose and relentless in persistence if we're going to see our dreams come true. Spectacular achievements are always preceded by unspectacular preparation. What about you? Are you taking the time to plan? To pray? To prepare? Never forget that the will to succeed is important. However, what is more important is the will to prepare. It's the will to go out and prepare for the sales call if you're in sales, train and build your muscles if you're an athlete, sharpen your skills if you're a teacher, manager, banker, pastor or plumber. Whatever profession you're in, the time you invest in preparation will determine if you will be ready when the opportunity for promotion or financial rewards comes your way. Remember, it wasn't raining when Noah built the ark!

4 Facts about Planning:

1. Planning will require your discipline, determination and follow-through.
2. Planning helps you focus and eliminate waste from your time.
3. Planning is a strategic exercise on paper that helps you think for tomorrow.
4. Planning will always help you discover the shortest path to your goal.

Here's a great Chinese proverb that every leader should remember when planning for the future:

"When planning for a year, plant corn. When planning for a decade, plant trees. When planning for life, train and educate people."

PERSISTENCE

There may be no characteristic more important in obtaining success than persistence. That special trait is found in all winners, because it relentlessly drives them toward excellence. Persistence also enables winners to bounce back after defeat, and whip any negative thought that approaches their mind. The ability to be persistent is in all great success stories because along the way, successful people all faced obstacles that tested their persistence. Remember the words of the former heavyweight boxing champion James Corbett who said, "Fight one more round. When your feet are so tired that you have to shuffle back to the center of the ring, fight one more round. When your arms are so tired that you can hardly lift your hands, fight one more round. When your nose is bleeding and your eyes are black, fight one more round, remembering that the man who always fights one more round is never whipped." Remember, success is getting up one more time than you fall!

Use What You've Been Given

Think about these words: "I do not choose to be a common man. It is my right to be uncommon if I can. I seek opportunity, not security. I do not wish to be kept a citizen, humbled and dulled by having the company look after me. I want to take the calculated risk, to dream and to build, to fail and to succeed. I refuse to barter incentive for a dole. I prefer the challenges of life to the guaranteed existence, the thrill of fulfillment to the stale of calm utopia. I will not trade freedom for beneficence, or dignity for a hand out. It is my heritage to think and act for myself, to enjoy the benefits of my creations, to face the world boldly and say, 'This I have done.'" He sounds like another man who wrote, "I have fought a good fight, I have finished my course, I have kept the faith."

What about you? Are you being persistent? Are you thinking bigger? Keeping the faith? Moving forward? Some may say, "But Julio, I'm disadvantaged." The fact is we all are in some capacity. Did you see the movie *Rain Man*? Dustin Hoffman plays a savant; a person who, in a sea of disabilities, has an island of genius inside. In the movie he's incredibly gifted with numbers. Other savants have amazing abilities in the arts and music. The truth is all of us arrived with a seed inside of us that must be watered, developed and grown. We've all been equipped and empowered to do something special. You have an island of genius inside of you. God has given you a gift. YOU must believe it, discover it, develop it, cherish it, protect it, use it and give it away!

And remember the words of George Bernard Shaw, "Progress is impossible without change, and those who cannot change their minds cannot change anything."

It Takes Faith

Many people fail because they quit too soon. They lose faith when the signs are against them. B.C. Forbes said, "History has demonstrated that the most notable winners usually encountered heartbreaking obstacles before they triumphed. They finally won because they refused to become discouraged by their defeats." Usually the only thing that stands between a person and what they want from life is the will to try it and the faith to believe it is possible. St. Augustine summed it up best when he said, "Faith is to believe what we do not see, and the reward of this faith is to see what we believe."

> *"He who walks with wise men will be wise,*
> *but the companion of fools will be destroyed."*
> —Proverbs 13:20

FRIENDSHIPS

Charles "Tremendous" Jones said that the only difference between the person you are today and the person you will be in five years will come from the books you read and the people you associate with. Every day you choose who your closest friends are and who you hang out with. If you choose negative friends, you are also choosing a negative attitude, which will eventually turn into a negative life. But when you spend time with positive people, you help yourself to see things in a better light and position yourself to win and succeed in life. Your best friends will always be those who bring out the best in you. Think about what your friends bring out in you, and if it's not your best, it might be time to make some changes. Here's an easy reminder: people are like elevators. They can bring you up or take you down.

Building and Protecting Relationships

One of the keys to living a great life is building and protecting relationships. It matters at home and in business. Yet, so many days we take for granted friendships and relationships that truly matter. Here are four concepts that will help you build and protect worthy relationships:

1. **Everyone needs reassurance of their worth.** At the end of the day we are all looking to be loved, appreciated and valued. Remind yourself throughout the day that each employee, co-worker, family member, client, etc. has encountered waves of criticism, self-doubt and condemnation that you can change. Your words of reassurance can be like water on their seeds of hope, potential and possibilities.

2. **There are four types of people in your life:** Those who add, subtract, multiply or divide. Your responsibility is to get away from those who subtract and divide. Get closer and pursue those who add and multiply to your life. Those who encourage you, challenge you, pray for you, support you and even correct you because they care. Those who do not increase you will eventually decrease you!

MENTAL SNACKS

3. **You're not the only one who struggles.** Others around you are hurting too. Be attentive to the silent cries of people close to you who may be drowning in the sea of discouragement, doubt and unbelief. Someone may open up and share the dream in their heart; make sure you listen. Someone else may need to hear an approving or encouraging word from you; make sure you say it.

4. **Keep your word.** Never promise what you cannot produce or follow up with. Make sure you review and fulfill any vows, promises or commitments you have made to anyone.

THE POWER OF IDEAS

Author Victor Hugo once said, "There's nothing more powerful than an idea whose time has come." Ideas are the greatest resource a successful person could ever have. And when you surround yourself with creative people, you're never at a loss for inspiring ideas. If you continually have good ideas, you have a better opportunity to reach your potential. How do you come up with ideas? Through believing you are capable of creative thinking. Most people use only a fraction of their brainpower and simply don't trust the rest. You are capable of generating good ideas—probably more than you think. First, realize that the only bad ideas are those that die without giving rise to other ideas. Second, realize that great ideas are often nothing more than the restructuring of what you already know.

Creativity Pays

Did you know that the greatest enemy of your creative powers is complacency? Creativity has been built into every one of us; it's part of our design. Creative people are constantly on the lookout for new ideas and new ways. They recreate and rearrange the present by finding novel ways to approach certain problems. Many times it's novel ideas that solve complex problems. And that is why you have to remember that, sometimes, novel ideas produce criticism from the masses. You may have never heard these lines but the creative people who decided to think out of the box did:

"You want to sell me a chicken recipe? You'll never get this idea off the ground, Colonel Sanders!"

"I'm sorry but your *Gone With the Wind* manuscript will have little public appeal."

"Watches with no hands? You're crazy!"

"How dumb do you think I am? You can't put music on a roll of tape."

History books are full of people who refused to bow down to criticism and who had enough faith to pursue their idea. Don't allow yourself to be satisfied with where you are. Be content (thankful for where you are and what you have), but don't be satisfied!

One last thought on creativity. Most people limit themselves by thinking unimaginatively. Stretching yourself beyond the usual and customary will not only help you grow but yield new experiences, ideas and unchartered territory. That's what makes the journey of life fun!

Your Foundation

In your preparation for building a strong foundation for success make sure you include these stones:

The worth of integrity
The privilege of working
The discipline of struggle
The power of prayer
The effectiveness of simplicity
The virtue of patience
The fruitfulness of perseverance
The joy of winning!

TIME FOR A CHECK-UP?

Did you hear about the guy named Bill who phoned his boss, disguised his voice and said, "I hear you're looking for a sharp, honest, hard-working young man." The boss replied, "Sorry, we already have someone like that. By the way, what's your name? Laughing, Bill replied, "This is Bill—and I was just checking up on myself!" When's the last time *you* checked up on yourself to see what kind of job you're doing? Are you diligent? Thoughtful? Loyal? Skillful? Teachable? Thorough? Fair? Honest? Cooperative? Positive? In today's world, the marketplace rewards those whose eyes are on the task, not the clock; it rewards people who think, "Why not," instead of, "Why me?" Remember, you can either endure or enjoy your job, but understand this—the place you work will never be any better than you make it!

Loving Your Job

In a national survey of 180,000 American workers, 80% indicated a dislike for their jobs. That is a sad reflection on an activity that absorbs a major portion of our lives. You need to remember that every day you're not just going to work as labor, but to build your life! Everyone should take a page from Thomas Edison's view of work: "I never did a day's work in my life. It was all fun." He believed that the purpose of work was joy and fulfillment. And while all work isn't fun, it is fun to have passion for your work and get paid to do it.

If you're going to have success at work you need to know what you are doing, like what you are doing, know why you are doing it and believe in what you are doing. It is important to get beyond the job description, paycheck, title, etc. and get engaged in your organization's mission and purpose. If you're not happy or passionate about your work, change your thinking or change your job but don't complain. The self-esteem, satisfaction and fulfillment you experience at work depend on you.

Here are some great words of wisdom from Art Linkletter regarding our work:

Do a little more than you're paid to;
Give a little more than you have to;
Try a little harder than you want to;
Aim a little higher than you think possible;
And give a lot of thanks to God for health, family and friends.

Sounds like a strong formula for success!

The Seed of Success

In your pursuit to succeed in all facets of your life never forget that persistence is the seed of success. If you start to get tired, remember the story of Charles Goodyear. Out of curiosity, Charles purchased a rubber-like substance while in India. He was told that rubber would be of great value for thousands of things. Charles began to invest his time, money and energy into his experiments (failing miserably) until his last dollar was spent. His family questioned his obsession with rubber and some of his friends thought he was going insane. But Goodyear was not as insane as most people thought. For five years, he battled with obstacles and adversities (just like you and I do daily). Eventually, his efforts were crowned with success. Out of hardships, defeat and some humiliation, Charles Goodyear succeeded. Now millions of people have purchased tires for their vehicles at Goodyear. He turned failure into success, defeat into victory. All because he persisted. Now it's your turn. Don't stop, don't give up, don't turn away, and in the coming days you will have victory!

"The world of tomorrow belongs to the
person who has the vision today."
—Robert Schuller

VISUALIZATION

Most people don't know what they want in life—what they want to be, where they want to go, what they want to see, share or do. Where are you headed? How are you going to get there? It doesn't matter where you started or where you are today. What matters is what you are doing right now. Too many people let life happen to them. Only a few decide for themselves what is going to happen to them. To just stay alive is not enough. You must have a picture of your life, because you can only do something you see. That's why people put pictures of a thin person on the refrigerator when they are trying to lose weight. It gives them a picture of what they want to be. When your heart decides on a destination, your mind will design a map to get there. While you can't decide when or how you are going to die, you can picture how you want to live!

Everybody Needs a Vision

Vision seems to be an elusive yet important life principle. Your vision describes the ideal future you want to have and live. It provides meaning and direction while forcing you to break through present limitations. Vision literally begins with imagination coupled with a belief that dreams can one day become a reality. David Schwartz, the author of *Thinking Big*, says, "You need to look at things not as they are, but as they can be. Visualization adds value to everything. A big thinker always visualizes what can be done in the future. He isn't stuck with the present."

What is the vision of your future? How do you plan to make the second half of this year different from the first? Next year different from years past? How will you be better tomorrow than you are today?

I love the story of the little girl who was drawing with her new set of 64 crayons. Her mother asked her what she was drawing. The little girl answered, "I'm drawing God." The mother responded, "Honey, nobody knows what God looks like." The child responded confidently, "They'll know when I'm finished." The lesson is a simple yet important one—people with a vision already know what the outcome is going to be even though no one has ever seen it before. Your vision is the blueprint of your ultimate achievements!

Have you looked at your goals lately? Are you 100% committed to achieving them? The person who believes they have made a commitment now knows there is a debt unpaid. This commitment fuels the fire that leads to effectiveness and productivity. The hard part comes after you have written down your goals and made a personal commitment to achieving them. You now have to discipline yourself to develop the habits that will lead you down the path of success. Simply put, successful people are able to form the habit of self-discipline and are motivated by satisfying results. Think about it, self-disciplined people are usually:

Enthusiastic
Resourceful
Persistent
Dedicated
Focused
Courageous

At this very moment, you have what it takes on the inside, but have you made the commitment? Are you self-disciplined? Remember, there are three kinds of people in the world. Those who make things happen, those who watch things happen and those who wonder what happened. Start making things happen...today!

"Stop looking at where you have been and
start looking at where you are going."
—Anonymous

YOUR MIND

Did you know that your mind is the drawing board for tomorrow's circumstances? What happens in your mind can happen in reality. The edge you are looking for today is in your mind. Your *attitude* can be your greatest *asset* or liability. Your attitude more than anything else will determine how far you go in life and how much you accomplish. What are you doing on a daily basis to keep your attitude positive? Are you reading something daily that is inspirational, spiritual, positive or motivational? What about the people you associate with? Are they positive or negative influences in your life? Researchers say that the average person has 40,000 thoughts a day and 80% are negative. Maintain a positive attitude in a negative world by renewing your mind daily!

No Worries

Recently I had the privilege of visiting Australia. I enjoyed the people and places tremendously. One thing I learned is that the Aussies have a line as part of their lingo that we as Americans ought to use and remember more often: No worries, mate!Everywhere I went I heard, "No worries." When I asked my driver if he could take me to a Starbucks, he said, "No worries." When I asked the concierge if he could help me with some reservations, he said, "No worries." When I asked my friend, Nick, if he could hold some seats at an event, he said, "No worries." I loved it. So many people spend their entire day worrying about things they have no control over. The word "worry" comes from an old Anglo-Saxon word that means "to choke" or "strangle." Every time we worry we are choking or strangling the life out of ourselves. I had a friend tell me years ago that worry was the opposite of prayer. I said, "What?" He said, "When you worry, it doesn't produce anything positive. Instead it creates stress and anxiety, but when you pray, positive results happen." Over the years I have tried to remember his advice and even though I'm still a recovering type-A personality, after visiting Sydney and seeing how chilled out the Aussies are, no worries sounds like a good philosophy to embrace! Think about it, mate!

Control

While there are many things you and I can't control, there are a couple of things you can control that greatly impact your life and your future. As you continue to pursue your goals and dreams, I want to remind you of the things you do control.

You can control:
1. Your free time
2. Your thoughts
3. Your attitude
4. Your tongue
5. Your commitments
6. Your role models and friends
7. Your spiritual faith
8. Your discretionary income
9. Your response to difficult times and people

Remember, we all live under the same sky but we all don't see the same horizons. Learn to lift your eyes and see the great possibilities!

> "The business of expanding your consciousness is not an option.
> Either you are expandable or you are expendable."
> —Robert Schuller

GROWING

Did you know that by the time most people are in their mid-30s, they've stopped acquiring any new skills or new attitudes? Does that surprise you? How long has it been since you acquired a new skill? How many new attitudes have you adopted lately? At work? At home? In your spiritual journey? With your personal finances? Are you stuck in a rut? Do you feel compelled to approach a problem the same way every time? Does a new idea make you put up your guard? Are you addicted to predictability? When was the last time you did something for the first time? Most people agree that growing is a good thing, yet few dedicate themselves to the process. Living and learning go hand in hand—just like living and breathing. The same hours and minutes that capture the wonder of a child can deepen the rut of an adult. The best way to keep from becoming complacent and continuing to grow is to make learning a lifetime commitment.

Keep Polishing Your Skills

The "Great" Stanley Marcus who helped build Neiman-Marcus Department Stores was not just a retailing genius but also had the ability to inspire growth in others. One of his favorite stories he shared with his employees was sent to me, and I want to share it with you. Marcus says:

"One of the most popular of my 'sermons' dealt with my comparison of human beings to brass. I cited a visit to the bridge of a naval vessel where the brass gleamed like gold. I asked the captain how often they had to shine the brass. He replied, 'Every day. The minute you stop polishing it, it starts to tarnish.' I correlated this incident to human beings, saying, 'None of us is made of gold, we're made of brass, but we can look like gold if we work hard at polishing ourselves as the sailor polishing the brass of the ship.'"

The lesson is a simple one. Apathy, routine, repetition, comfort zone and lack of challenge are all life tarnishers. Putting forth the shining effort that gives your talents, potential and dreams their intended gleam and sparkle can return the luster. Keep polishing your skills and talent because the moment you stop, your brass will start to tarnish!

One last thought: Healthy, growing, fulfilled people are always striving to expand their spiritual, mental, social, financial and physical capacities to help others.

LIFE

Stop for a minute and figure out the cost of the phrase "wait a minute." For example, if you earn approximately $25,000 a year, every minute you have to wait costs 5 cents; at $50,000 a year, this figure doubles to nearly 10 cents a minute. If you earn $500,000 a year, your time is worth more than $1 dollar a minute. The point is simply that time is valuable. Every day you can either invest or spend your time. Every morning credits you with 86,400 seconds. Every night it rules off as lost whatever amount you have failed to invest. It carries over no balance and allows no overdrafts. If you fail to use today's deposit, the loss is yours. There is no going back, no drawing against tomorrow. Invest your seconds so that they will give you the utmost in health, happiness and success!

Do You Have What It Takes?

Watching Lance Armstrong win his seventh consecutive Tour de France and learning about his commitment, training and focus made me think about how much potential every person has but never fulfills. Yes, Lance may be another special athlete in his sport, as Michael Jordan was in basketball, but like all the great ones, he did the little things that make the biggest difference.

Did you know…

Lance pays attention to every single detail?

He trained, planned, did research, and weighed his food every day to maintain proper nutrition?

He sought out the best counsel when he needed help with anything?

He studied the best in their fields, including Michael Jordan, Wayne Gretzky and Tiger Woods, for inspiration?

He greeted every morning with enthusiasm?

He believes anything can be done with hard work?

He was 33 years old and out-cycled a bunch of 20-something competitors?

He brings a single-minded commitment to work every day?

   His preparation, attitude and ability to focus are uncommon. His training, techniques, commitment and results are uncommon. However, all the things he did to prepare to win, are common things that you and I can do to win in the game of life. What are you doing to improve your performance at work? Do you plan and prepare every day? Do you possess a single-minded commitment to your work? You can either prepare today or repair tomorrow. The choice is yours!

THE FUTURE

A boy named Tommy had a particularly hard time in school. He constantly asked questions and was never able to keep up with the other kids in his class. His teacher finally gave up on him and told his mother that he couldn't learn and would never amount to much. But Tommy's mother was a nurturer; she believed in him. She taught him at home, and each time he failed, she gave him hope and encouraged him to keep trying. Whatever happened to Tommy? Well, eventually he grew up and became an inventor with more than 1,000 patents, including the phonograph and the first electric light bulb. His full name was Thomas Edison. Your words have power, so use every opportunity to teach faith, confidence, life and hope to other people. When people have hope and encouragement, there's no telling how far they can go!

You Have to Endure

Endurance is the quality of champions in sports, business and life! If you're going to live an uncommon life, you have to keep believing, keep reaching, keep going and keep focused. Patience and perseverance are the golden keys that unlock the greatness of individuals. Think about it. The acorn becomes an oak tree. Ordinary people become extraordinary leaders. Average salespeople become extraordinary producers. Small companies become successful enterprises. All great achievements will require time and endurance. The uncommon leader recognizes that the adversities and challenges he confronts will produce long-term rewards. There are several steps you and I can take to make sure we endure and extend our lives.

1. **Stay active**—Exercise gives you energy and mental alertness.
2. **Be optimistic**—Physiologically…happiness is a state of mind that is healthy for the body.
3. **Plan significant events**—You will always have something to look forward to.
4. **Confront adversity**—John Wooden once told me, "Adversity will always make you stronger if you learn from it." He was right. Adver-

sity and problems are an ongoing integral part of living.

5. **Laugh and have fun**—Don't take yourself or your work too seriously. Life is too short not to enjoy!

Maximize Your Potential

There isn't a ruler, yardstick or measuring tape in the world large enough to compute the strength and capabilities of the giant who is fast asleep within you. Its size and power are unlimited. Its force is that of a million dynamos. Its tireless energy is beyond all comprehension. It's the giant of your untapped potential; it's your ability to unfold, to develop and to grow. It will continue to lie there peacefully asleep until you decide to wake it. Like the desert lacking water, too often people endure shortages in their lives, when all they have to do is simply open the valves—the valves of attitudes, habits, focus and a plan of action to achieve what is lacking. The giant who sleeps in all people only awakens when they take control of their abilities, talent and skills. They tap their potential by taking action in a personal way. So can you.

"It is often hard to distinguish between the
hard knocks in life and those of opportunity."
—Fred Phillips

DIFFICULTIES

I remember the year that two hurricanes hit South Louisiana in a four-week span. It caused havoc in the lives of thousands of people like few in America have ever seen or experienced. Having had many of my own family members affected (some lost everything they had) and hundreds of friends impacted, I can't help but dwell on the power of hope! When you trust in God, when you live in America, when you have an eternal perspective, when you resolve and develop the capacity to keep moving forward, you create opportunity. I believe we can turn crises into creative opportunities, defeats into successes and frustration into fulfillment with our great invisible weapons: faith, hope, love and commitment!

No matter what difficulty you're facing today, only *you* can determine the quality of life you will live moving forward. Think about it:

• You can't control the weather, but you can control the atmosphere that surrounds you.

• You can't control the length of your life, but you can control its width and depth.

• You can't control the contour of your countenance, but you can control its expression.

• You can't control what happened yesterday, but you can make decisions today that will give you the future you want tomorrow.

Life itself can't give you joy and happiness, unless you really pursue it. Everyone is given time and space, and it's up to you to fill it with the right people and attitudes!

Overcoming Adversity

J.C. Penney once said, "I would have never amounted to anything were it not for adversity. I was forced to come up the hard way." Most people don't handle adversity very well, because they don't understand its advantages. What happens in life, happens to all of us. Whether you're black, white, Hispanic, Chinese, male, female, rich, poor, young or old, adversity is not prejudiced. It visits us all. Adversity is part of life, so let me help you change your thinking about it. Recognize that adversity will force you to dig for more accurate information and to pause for introspection. What lessons are you learning? What did you learn from this experience? Adversity reveals the depth of friendships. Who are your real friends? Adversity also strengthens you and helps you decide what you really believe. Remember, it's not what happens to you that matters, it's what you do with what happens to you that counts!

"Instead of giving myself reasons why I can't, I give myself reasons why I can."

—Unknown

ENCOURAGEMENT

Have you ever had someone encourage you when you felt low or down in the dumps? Do you remember how that encouragement rejuvenated you, giving you a fresh desire to persevere? Growing up, one of the greatest gifts my mother always gave me—and still gives me—is encouragement. It is impossible to receive too much warmth, caring, affection and affirmation. Kindness strengthens, love restores, affection heals and affirmation comforts those who are listening. Those who offer encouragement to others will themselves be encouraged. We all need encouragement, especially after our greatest defeats when doubt and discouragement set in. Be like oxygen to the soul of those around you today. Encouragement fortifies the soul. Who can you encourage today?

Guidepost for Success

There's a cool book titled, *The Traveler's Gift.* In it, author Andy Andrews offers and identifies seven attitudes that make the difference between success and failure.

If you read the book it will speak to your heart, inspire your thinking and motivate your life. Think about these seven guideposts for success:

1. Remember, the buck stops here. Be responsible for your past and future.
2. Seek wisdom. Be a servant to others.
3. Be a person of action. Seize this moment—now!
4. Have a decided heart. Your destiny is assured.
5. Today, choose to be happy. Be the possessor of a grateful spirit.
6. Greet this day with a forgiving spirit.
7. Persist without exception. Be a person of great faith.

You'll want to read and digest these principles on a regular basis. They will make the difference between success and failure. Don't look at where you've been, but stay focused on where you are going!

Success Is a Collection of Relationships

Think about it. Without clients, a lawyer has no career. Without patients, a doctor has no future. Without a composer, a singer has nothing to say. Without players, a coach has no one to lead; without customers a retailer has no business; and without the right relationship, you won't be fulfilled. Relationships provide us with a great opportunity to motivate others, help them grow, provide encouragement and enhance the quality of their lives. And in return, we will experience the same.

Your future is connected to people. Hang around successful people. Network where your best customers and prospects go. Join the right associations and organizations. Stay away from miserable, negative people. Those who are going nowhere but are always criticizing, complaining and whining. There is a great Proverb that says, "He that walks with the wise shall become wise, but a companion of fools shall be destroyed." The point is to be selective about your friendships.

CHANGE

Change is inevitable, but growth is optional. There are only three things you can do with change: You can fight it, ignore it or embrace it. If you fight change in your organization or life, you'll become discouraged or discontented and you'll never reach your full potential. If you ignore change, you'll be swept away by your colleagues or competition. However, if you learn to embrace change, mold it and understand that it is part of life, you'll be on your way to enjoying the journey of life. If you can't change, you won't grow, and if you're not growing, you're not really living. How many books have you read this past year? Most people are willing to pay $25 for a good meal, but they won't spend a dime for a good book or a CD that can help them change, improve and learn. When you are through changing, you're through. Growth must be a priority or it will never happen.

Shift Happens

Have you ever noticed how people almost freak out when you begin to talk about change or changing things? I even know a CEO who, because his employees got nervous every time he talked about change in his organization, said any time they were going to change things he would use the word "shift" instead. He would say, "We are going to be shifting things around here." For some reason it was softer on the ears of employees.

The reality is that whether we tag it as change or shift, it is going to happen. It can happen to us or happen because of us. Today I want to challenge you to be an agent of change where you use your talents, skills and opportunities to shape your world and the world around you in a more positive way. You must be on a relentless pursuit to get to the next level at whatever you do and that will take shifting your thinking, your strategy, your priorities and your life constantly. That is one of the ways you enhance your life, produce results, become fulfilled and impact your community and industry.

If you think I'm off base on this challenge, just remember the Apple

Computer television ad that came out in 1997. The great line in that commercial was, "The people who are crazy enough to think they can change the world are the ones who do." They were right!

More Thoughts on Change

"It is not the strongest of the species that survive, nor the most intelligent, but the one most responsive to change."
—*Unknown*

"Those who expect moments of change to be comfortable and free of conflict have not learned their history."
—*Joan Wallach Scott*

"If you're in a bad situation, don't worry, it'll change. If you're in a good situation, don't worry, it'll change."
—*John A. Simone, Sr.*

> "No life ever grows great until it is focused,
> dedicated and disciplined."
> —Harry Fosdick

TODAY

How are you living right now? Are you enjoying today? Read these words carefully. *Just for today*, I'll experience and enjoy each hour to the fullest and not try to tackle my whole life's problems at once. *Just for today*, I'll try to improve my mind by learning more. I'll read something that requires effort, thought and commitment. *Just for today*, I'll look my best, speak well and be considerate of others. *Just for today*, I won't find fault or try to change or improve anyone but myself. *Just for today*, I'll have a plan and a goal. I might not follow them exactly, but I'll have them nonetheless. By doing this, I'll save myself from two enemies—hurry and indecision. *Just for today*, I'll exercise my character. I'll do something good for someone and keep it a secret. *Just for today*, I won't be afraid to love or to risk. *Just for today*, take a good look around you and be thankful you live in America today.

Excellence Every Day

Do you stamp your work with excellence every day? Would co-workers or clients describe your work as excellent? If you got arrested today and were accused of being a person of excellence, would there be enough evidence to convict you?

People who are considered to be excellent in their field have some common characteristics, and I'd like to share four of them with you:

1. They are **never satisfied** with average—They understand that good is the enemy of great.

2. They are **committed** to excellence—It is a decision they have made in their heads and hearts. They measure their value not against others but against their own potential.

3. They pay attention to **details**—They get the concept that if you do the little things well, the big ones tend to fall into place.

MENTAL SNACKS

4. They perform and produce with **consistency**—They give it every-thing they have…every time. If 99.9% effort were good enough, then 132,000 computers purchased this year would not work, 22,000 checks would be deducted from the wrong bank accounts in the next hour and 12 babies would be given to the wrong parents every day of the year. The lesson is a simple one. Never settle for less than doing your best at everything you do…every day of your life!

PASSION

If you're going to have long-term success in your career, you must pursue your passion, not your pension. When you pursue your passion, you'll be inspired to learn as much as you can and to gain as many skills as you can, and then you'll be sought after for your quality service and dedication to excellence. Your passion will make you oblivious to quitting time and to the length of your workday. You'll wake up every morning with the passion of pursuit, but not with the pursuit of money. Those who do more than they're paid for are always sought out for their services. Their passion qualifies them for promotion and financial rewards. Their name and work outlive them. If what you love begins to consume your mind, your thoughts, your conversations, your schedule, get ready for extraordinary success and results. You will only have significant success with something that you have passion for!

Think about It

I believe one of the major keys in the success or failure of any organization boils down to passion. Are you operating from passion? If you are, the odds are you're going to succeed. If you believe in what you are doing, it becomes contagious and spreads to others. Passion is all about the energy and attitude you bring to your family, job and life. Are you spreading the fire?

Four quick keys to keep an edge in life:

1. Make sure you practice what you preach and preach what you practice. Show that you care—by attitude, word and action. Practice the correct way, not the easy way.

2. Do what you can do today. Don't wait for tomorrow because you never know if it will come.

3. Deliver more than customers and others expect. Deliver value not mediocrity.

94

4. Be grateful and thankful every morning you get up from bed. As a friend of mine always says, if you did not wake up this morning with a white chalk mark outlining your body, then you're alive. Celebrate your life!

Optimism and Passion

Do you know optimism is not about the way you feel but about the way you think? Motivation tends to be based on how you feel about something. Optimism is based on how you think about a situation. You can actually learn to think optimistically. Optimists believe good events are going to continue and that bad events are transitory. Thomas Edison continues to be a great example for all of us. He could have said, "I have failed 10,000 times." Instead, he said, "I have successfully found 10,000 ways that will not work." That is an optimist.

When you begin to think like an optimist you generate energy! The result is eagerness to continue to grow, pursue, invest and keep going. That energy turns into passion and passion leads to success! Remember, opportunities and solutions are all around us if you just think the right way.

ACTION

Suppose you had five birds sitting on a wire and three of them decided to fly. How many birds would you have left on the wire? Five birds is the correct answer. Making a decision to fly without acting on the decision is a waste of energy. The momentum to do something about our decisions is energized by action! To become successful, you must be a person of action. Many people "know" what they are supposed to do, but to "know" is not enough. You must know and do. Nolan Bushell, the founder of Atari, was once asked about his entrepreneurial success. He responded, "The critical ingredient is getting off your butt and doing something." It's as simple as that. A lot of people have ideas, but there are few who decide to do something about them now. Not tomorrow. Not next week. Today. The true entrepreneur is a doer, not a dreamer. Don't let your ideas, dreams or good intentions sit idly on a wire. Take action today!

We Need a Revolution!

I can't stop thinking about the revolution that is beginning. The revolution that our community, our country and this world needs. A revolution is a "drastic and far-reaching change in ways of thinking and behaving." If you think about it, the industrial revolution was also a cultural revolution.

Today we are living in times where we need one more than ever. There is a revolution that needs to occur. One that is peaceful but powerful. One that brings purpose and meaning to people's lives. One that strengthens their families and energizes their work. These are unprecedented times of change. I know the word "revolution" may scare some, but it is time for action! Action erases doubts, fears, anxieties and worries. It capitalizes on mistakes and turns them into positive lessons and influences. Things don't just happen; things are made to happen—it starts with you. Think about it:

We need more ACTION and less lip service.

We need more LEADERSHIP and less management.
We need MORE PERSONAL RESPONSIBILITY and less blame.
We need TO THINK BIG, not small.
We need more TRUTH and fewer pretenses.
We need to have more FUN instead of whining.
We need more COOL and less dull (cool begets cool).
We need more PASSION and less passivity.
We need more TRANSFORMATION and less status quo.
We need more GRATITUDE and less complaining.
We need MORE EXCELLENCE and less mediocrity.

What are you waiting for? Send this mental snack to all your friends, clients and vendors. Spread the fire and join the revolution!

"If you don't know where you are going,
you will probably end up somewhere else."
—Laurence Peter

GOALS

One of the major causes of failure is the unwillingness to take time to set goals. Goals are the alpha and omega of success, the beginning and the end. Goals create your road map for achievement. Most people have heard about goals, yet few practice this powerful discipline. Goal setting takes time, discipline, courage and patience. Why should you make goal-setting a lifetime habit? Goals give you a sense of purpose, something concrete to focus on. That focus will positively impact your actions. The future doesn't get better by hoping; it gets better by having a plan. Which did you plan for more, your wedding or your marriage? Which do you plan for more, your vacation or your life? No one ever accomplishes anything worthwhile without a goal. Above all, keep in mind that the most important thing about goals is making some!

New Beginnings

Do you have high hopes and ambitious plans for the future? I certainly do. Yet many times what we deemed the year of great opportunities turns out to be a year of disappointment. One recent study found that 70% of people couldn't keep their New Year resolutions even through the month of January, much less the whole year. Most people begin a New Year with all sorts of resolutions, expectations and hopes. I want to challenge you to not only make goals and plans for your work life, but also for the other critical areas of your life. Remember, if you ignore one, the wheels in the journey of life get out of balance:

1. **Spiritual life**—Don't ignore this facet of your life. Feed your soul and strengthen your faith.

2. **Family life**—Nourish the relationships in your life. The proof of your love is the investment of your time.

3. **Physical**—Your body is a temple. What should be your weight based on your height and body composition? According to a recent study

done by researchers with the National Institute of Health, most people gain five pounds or more during the holidays.

4. **Financial**—Make sure you save, give and invest in your future. Do you have a plan?

5. **Intellectual**—How do you plan to grow this year? The primary way you bring value to your clients, company and marketplace is by your knowledge base. How many books will you read? How many seminars or classes will you attend to continue to learn more?

Some people start the year hoping things will get better. Hope is not a strategy, but clearly outlining your vision for the future is!

> "One is not born into the world to do everything, but to do something."
> —Henry David Thoreau

REGRETS

A friend once told me that funerals were for the living, not the dead. He was right. It is a time for those who are living to reflect on their limited days left on this earth. Make sure you maximize the moments and opportunities.

Over the past few months I have had a couple of family members and friends pass away. As I thought about their lives, I reflected upon my own life. I don't want to look back at the end of my life and have regrets. For the most part, regrets are a function of lost opportunities and poor choices. The way to avoid regrets is to be pro-active in every facet of your life (work, family, spiritual, health, financial, etc.). The lesson I've learned from older people is that regret plays with your mind and tortures your soul. So as you look ahead to your future, bury the past today. You can't build your future on regret; you can only wallow in it. Learn from your past but don't live there. The best way to turn regrets into opportunities is to set up personal goals that will redeem the regrets. It has always worked for me, and I'm sure it can work for you.

Today, write down three to five things you'd like to accomplish this year personally and professionally. Be specific. It's easier to accomplish your goals if they are detailed instead of vague. Think and dream big! Establish goals that will light the way for the life you deserve to live. The only place you'll find people with no problems and no goals is the cemetery. Let's live with no regrets!

Life Is about the Journey

In his essay "The Station," Robert Hastings writes about how we see ourselves on a long train trip that spans the continent. As we look out the windows, we drink in the passing scenes—children waving, cattle grazing, city skylines and village halls. But uppermost in our minds is the final destination. On a certain day, we'll pull into the station, bands will play, and flags will wave. Once we arrive, we believe, so many wonderful dreams will come true. Restlessly we pace the aisles, despising the minutes, waiting for that station. "When we reach the station, that will be it," we cry. When I buy my Mercedes. When I get married. When I've paid off the mortgage. Waiting for the station. But sooner or later we realize that the true joy of life is not the destination, but the journey itself. "So stop pacing the aisles and counting the miles," Hastings writes. Enjoy the journey. The station will come soon enough.

ATTITUDE

A few years ago a Fortune 500 study found that 94% of all executives surveyed attributed their success more to attitude than any other factor. If you want to go far in your career you must have a good attitude. Your attitude affects more than just your ability to succeed in business. It affects every aspect of your life—even your health. A study was conducted of 57 cancer patients who had undergone mastectomies at King's College Hospital in London, England. Research showed that, of the patients with a positive attitude when they were diagnosed with cancer, 7 out of 10 were still alive 10 years later. But of the patients who felt a sense of hopelessness during diagnosis, 8 out of 10 had died. A good attitude is the fuel that will make your journey down the road of life a long and successful one.

Your Best Thoughts

We live in times where negativity runs rampant, arrows of discouragement bombard our minds and doubt tries to penetrate our lives daily. While many of life's circumstances are uncontrollable, our responsibility is to choose our responses, our thoughts and our attitude. Situations may color your view of life, but you have been given the power to choose what the color will be.

For those tempted not to read on and endure another sermon on positive thoughts, stick with me. The thoughts you think daily have a profound influence on your attitude toward God, your family, your work and your future. As you seek to elevate your life to the next level, think about these maxims capable of pole-vaulting you higher:

1. A positive attitude is a *choice* and it's *free* (you get to choose yours every day).

2. Your attitude affects the *quality of your life* (a positive attitude will help you do everything better than a negative attitude will).

3. It's not your age that counts; it's your *attitude* (whether you're 29, 59 or 79, you can live your best life now—it begins in your mind).

4. Attitude is a catalyst for *productivity* (when our attitude is right, our abilities reach a maximum effectiveness and positive results follow).

It's all a matter of perspective. Some people see the positives and opportunities in every situation, while others go through life seeking their induction into the negative attitude hall of fame. Ultimately, the little difference that makes the biggest difference in your life is your attitude!

ENERGY

Did you know that every human being is empowered with four types of energy? Each one of us has been given physical energy, mental energy, spiritual energy and emotional energy. Your performance, health, happiness and longevity on this earth are grounded in the skillful management of energy. While the number of hours in a day is fixed, the quantity and quality of energy available to us is not. We need to know when to effectively charge hard and when to renew and replenish our energy. To be fully engaged and become all we were meant to be, we must be physically energized, emotionally connected, spiritually aligned and mentally focused. Here are three quick thoughts on the benefits and management of your energy:

1. When we do not have passion for our work or when we're occupied doing something our hearts and minds are not interested in, we get fatigued. However, when we engage our whole heart, mind and body, we get energized.

2. Every one of our thoughts, emotions and behaviors has an energy consequence for better or for worse. That's the reason it is healthier to be a positive thinker than a negative thinker. Negative thinking affects your attitude, your health and your life.

3. We were not meant to do more than we were meant to do. The reality is you can't do it all. That is why you have to prioritize your focus in life and make sure that you have fuel in your tank physically, spiritually, emotionally and mentally. Exercising, weekend getaways, prayer, loving relationships and learning new things all contribute to the replenishment of your soul.

At the end of our life we should be able to say, we ran our race, fought our fight and finished our course—strong!

Attitude Counts Too

One day two men went into the hospital at about the same time, after suffering similar heart attacks. One of the men grew depressed and irritable. He felt betrayed by his own body and saw his affliction as a sign of weakness. His attitude was sour and he cursed his fate. The other man took it in stride. He kidded with everyone who came to visit him and refused to be brought down by his plight. Instead, he spent a good bit of his time cheering up other patients and chatting with the staff. The first man grew weak and frail. The other man left the hospital in good health and resumed his old life quickly. The way we face life has a lot to do with how good we feel about it. If you are negative, then life will be a burden, but if you are positive, life will seem like the greatest gift you have ever known. Your living is determined not so much by what life brings to you as by the attitude you bring to life!

LAUGHING

Many years ago, Norman Cousins was diagnosed as being terminally ill. He was only given six months to live and was told that his chances for recovery were extremely limited. He realized that the worry, depression and anger in his life probably contributed and perhaps helped cause the disease. He wondered, "If illness can be caused by negativity, can wellness be created by positivism?"

He then decided to make an experiment of himself. He rented all the comedy movies he could find. He read funny stories and asked his friends to call him any time they heard or did anything funny. He laughed so much that he found relief from his pain. Over time, he fully recovered from his illness and lived another 20 years. (His journey is detailed in a book, *Anatomy of an Illness*.) He credits visualization, the love of his family and friends, and laughter for his recovery.

Are you laughing enough? Are you having fun and taking time to laugh? There have been hundreds of studies on the subject of laughter and life. The conclusions are all the same. Laughter has a curative effect on the body, mind and emotions. That's why I laugh as often as I can. There is nothing better than a good belly laugh—indulge in one as often as you can!

Optimism

Abraham Lincoln said, "An optimist is one who sees opportunity in every difficulty. A pessimist is one who sees difficulty in every opportunity." He was right. Optimism is an attitude, an outlook and a perception all in one. There is an organization directed toward optimistic people, as well as toward pursuing change in a pessimistic society. The members have an international creed that is worth repeating: "Be so strong that nothing can disturb your peace of mind. Talk health, happiness and prosperity to every person you meet. Make all your friends feel there is something in them worthwhile. Look at the sunny side of everything and make your optimism come true." You see, adversity or difficulty can make you tender or tough, bitter or better—it all depends on you. Think only the best, work only for the best, do only your best and expect only the best!

"I cannot give you the formula for success, but I can give you
the formula for failure: try to please everybody."

—Hebert Swope

GET WHAT YOU WANT

Did you know you can have anything you want? You just can't have everything you want. No matter how smart or powerful a human being can be, everyone has a few significant limitations. Think about it:

1. We can only be in one place (physically) one moment at a time.
2. We only have 24 hours each day and 365 days a year.
3. We all only have so many years on the earth. (Somewhere between zero and 120 years.)

The list can go on and on. So contrary to some TV commercials, positive thinking gurus and self-help books, you can't have it all. There's just too much "it all" and not enough time on the earth. The good news is we can have anything we want. The only limitations on "anything" are: Can it be gotten by anyone and, is it available? If the answer to those two questions is yes, then it's there for you as well. It all starts with your faith and belief system. It takes several practical steps to get what you want, and I want to share some with you this week and some next week. Here are the first few:

1. Become *obsessed!* Focus your thoughts, prayers, mind and attention on what you want. It must become an obsession. (Tiger Woods is obsessed with golf; Henry Ford was obsessed with the automobile; Thomas Edison with inventions, etc.)

2. Be a *fanatic!* Get fired up about getting and having what you want. (Great marriage, more income, successful career, health, etc.)

3. Visualize and imagine yourself doing or having whatever it is you desire. (Before I write a book, I come up with a title and have a cover designed. Then I place it on my mirror and look at it every day.)

4. Write down exactly what you want. Be detailed and precise.

5. Turn away, extract and remove everything and anything opposing your goal.

It starts with these fundamentals. Next week I'll share a few more practical things you can do to fulfill your dreams.

"Press on. Obstacles are seldom the same
size tomorrow as they are today."
—Robert Schuller

OBSTACLES

You are as big as you think. If you don't believe that statement, then read this story of John and Greg Rice. These twins were born as dwarfs. Shortly after birth, they were abandoned by their parents because the couple wouldn't accept the responsibility of raising a pair of clubfoot dwarfs. Nine months later a couple took them in. But while in grade school, both of the adults died. Still, the twins maintained an unbelievable, positive attitude and made a goal in high school that they would some day be millionaires. They started out as door-to-door salesmen and soon ended up owning the company and becoming the millionaires that they dreamed of as youngsters. John and Greg didn't let the obstacle of their physical abilities interfere with their will and drive to succeed. Remember, the difference between a successful person and others is not a lack of height, but rather a lack of will!

Don't Give Up

Did you know that difficulties usually bring out your best qualities and make greatness possible in your life? Remarkable performances in business, sports or the classroom usually take place because an individual subscribes to the philosophy of "It's always too early to give up." Think about it. When you're going through a tough time, but you continue to move forward in the midst of the adversity, you learn some of the greatest lessons in your life. You strengthen your resolve. And, you move steadfastly toward your goals.

Let's look at sales for an example. Studies reveal that 58%—more than half—of all salespeople quit completely after a single call on a prospect. Another 20% make two calls before giving up, and 7% make three calls. The remaining 22% make five calls or more, and these are the superstars who make mucho money because they produce about 75% of the business. And there lies the lesson. It's not what happens to you, but what you do after it happens, that makes the big difference in your selling life. It's the salesperson who uses difficulty, not the ones who *avoid* it, who grows and goes to the top in the company.

And it's the exact same thing in your personal life. We all have issues and storms in our lives that we must overcome. Just like an oak tree grows strong in contrary winds and diamonds are made under pressure, our lives only become complete and fulfilled after we have persevered!

Great thought from B.C. Forbes, who said, "History has demonstrated that the most notable winners usually encountered heartbreaking obstacles before they triumphed. They won because they refused to become discouraged by their defeats."

A Common Obstacle

The killer of human potential is the comfort zone. Someone once said, "Many people have died while still living, because they got stuck in their comfort zone." They became complacent at work, in their marriage, with their health. Our society encourages us to seek comfort. Most products and services advertised are designed to make us more comfortable and less challenged. And yet, only challenge causes growth. Only challenge tests our skills and makes us better. Only challenge and the self-motivation to take on the challenge will transform us. Colin Wilson said, "When a butterfly has emerged, it can never turn back into a caterpillar." It is up to you to constantly look for challenges to motivate yourself. Use your comfort zones to rest in, not to live in. Use them to relax and restore your energy as you mentally prepare for your next challenge. Remember, if it were easy, everyone would be doing it!

> "The distance between yesterday's regrets and
> tomorrow's dreams is today's opportunities."
> —Unknown

GOALS

Most people don't understand that the reason they're not achieving or getting what they want in life is because their major goals are too vague and too small. And therefore, they have no energy or power. Your major goal will only be reached if it excites and energizes your imagination. It gets you up in the morning. You can taste it, feel it and smell it. You've got it clearly pictured in your mind. You've got it written down and you look at it every day. The great Walt Disney left us many wonderful things: Disneyland, Walt Disney World, Mickey Mouse, the great animated films. But I believe his greatest gift was the summing up he did of his life's work: "If you can dream it," he said, "you can do it." Your major goal is a dream that motivates, drives and inspires you. Think of it this way: it's not what a goal is that matters, it's what a goal does!

Don't Get in a Rut

I recently had the privilege to be part of a seminar where world-class speaker and minister from Australia, Christine Caine, spoke. She was dynamic, but more importantly, she shared some nuggets of wisdom that can help all of us in our leadership and personal growth. Here are a few:

1. **Age is an attitude of the heart.** That is why you find some people who are 30 that act like they are 70, and some that are 70 that act like they are 30. It is all about your attitude. It was William Wallace in the movie *Braveheart* who said, "Every man dies, but not every man lives." It is all about the attitude you bring to your family, your work and your life. Make sure yours is filled with gusto!

2. **Your passion must grow.** You've got to make a decision (must be intentional) not only to sustain your passion for life and work, but also to increase your passion. (Passion = internal enthusiasm) Passion is an issue of your heart. For example, your marriage starts off with passion and then turns into obligation. In order for our mar-

riage, work, etc. not to just be an obligation, we must continue to stretch, change, develop and grow. That is what will keep you going. Don't allow yourselves to get into a rut. When was the last time you stretched yourself? When was the last time you took a risk? When was the last time you did something for the first time?

3. **Your outer world and inner world must be aligned.** In other words, you can't separate your personal life and professional life. You are who you are. If you're committed to integrity, honesty and excellence, it will show up in every area of your life. If you give a great talk but don't walk the talk, there will come a time when your life will implode. Let's make sure that we marry our inner and outer worlds so there is alignment. Remember, it's never too late.

4. **"Suck the marrow out of life."** That's a great line from the movie *Dead Poets Society*, but one that we should all strive for. The purpose of life is not to get through the day, but to take from the day. If you woke up this morning and there is no white chalk around your body, it means you're alive! So go for it!

The older people get, the harder it gets to grow. That is why you must continue to dream and have goals to keep you growing. The greatest benefit to your family or your company is that you grow. Remember, mistakes happen and adversity will visit us all. Don't look at where you have been but start looking at (focus on) where you are going!

"Waste neither time, nor money but make the best use of both."

—Benjamin Franklin

REST

A tired mind rarely makes good decisions. Fatigue can be very costly. Yet many people who are capable of managing companies and developing complex budgets don't have the sense to know when they need a break, or how to use their resources without depleting them. If you're wise, you won't just put appointments on your calendar, you'll schedule some "down time" too. Well-timed rest restores your energy and maintains your abilities, so that you can function at full capacity. Many people are like the driver who's so concerned about where he's going and how fast he can get there that he doesn't notice that the engine's knocking, the tires are losing air and the gas tank is almost empty. Then, when the car breaks down, he asks, "What happened?" Life is demanding. In fact, the more you succeed, the more people will demand of you, but it is up to you to rest and repair yourself. Work hard, but play just as enthusiastically!

Who's in Charge of Your Time?

Recently, I went on a great trip to Cal-a-Vie, a World Class Health Spa and Resort in the outskirts of San Diego. It is one of the finest places you could ever go if you want to rejuvenate your soul, cleanse your mind, exercise your body and eat the best tasting health meals on the planet. Their staff and customer service is second to none. You can check it out at www.cal-a-vie.com.

After being gone for four days, I returned to a plethora of phone messages, junk e-mails and correspondence. Here's the thought that hit me. One of the evil side effects of technology is the proliferation of junk communication. The easier it has become to communicate, the more unnecessary and poorly thought out communication has increased. Have you noticed? All of this eats up your time, creates stress and, for some people, decreases their productivity.

Too many people have given up control of their time to others. Here are a couple of ideas to guard your time and schedule:

MENTAL SNACKS

1. Quit being compulsive about your e-mails. If you're constantly checking your e-mail, compulsively or as they arrive, you're headed for trouble. Instead, have a system, such as checking your e-mails twice in the morning and twice in the afternoon. Deal only with those that are urgent, and set the others aside for a time when you can delete, respond or forward. (I know we now have Treos and Blackberrys, which is more the reason to have a personal system.)

2. Incoming calls and drop in visitors should all be treated the same with an ending time in mind. You probably won't win any social awards, but you'll have shorter, more purposeful conversations and meetings. Too many people have a way of stretching out conversations to fill whatever amount of time you give them.

3. Stay focused on your work. When you are visibly busy conquering your tasks for the day, people will have less of a tendency to interrupt you. If you are sitting around chit-chatting, looking relaxed, comfortable, or worse, not working, you're an easy target for others to come up and eat up your valuable time.

The lesson is a simple one. You must schedule and guard your time carefully. You're in charge of your life and time, no one else!

> "Warmth, kindness and friendship are the most yearned for commodities in the world. The person who can provide them will never be lonely."
> —Ann Landers

RELATIONSHIPS

Napoleon conquered the world, yet when he died in exile on the island of St. Helena, he was alone and forsaken by all who knew him best. His wife went back to her father. His best friend deserted him without even saying goodbye. Two of his most trusted marshals openly insulted him, and even his faithful servants who slept outside his bedroom door left him. Why? Because he was self-centered! The people around him felt used but never appreciated. What a lesson—especially for people who think "they don't need others" or "they don't have time to waste on people." If you reach all your goals, but lose the people who matter the most in the process, what have you gained? Imagine having a story to tell, but nobody to listen, something to celebrate, but nobody to celebrate with. Don't let it happen to you. What you deposit into your relationships today is ALL you'll have to draw on later.

Rules for Dealing with People

Have you ever had a conversation with another person where the entire time they are so busy talking about themselves, that they don't hear what you have to say? Or have you ever been called on by a salesperson, and they are so busy talking about their product and their company that they haven't even taken a moment to ask you about yours? These people have the "me-itis" disease. They need to heed the words of Dale Carnegie who said, "you can make more friends in two months by becoming interested in other people than you can in two years by trying to get people interested in you."

A Carnegie Foundation study once showed that only 15% of a businessperson's success could be attributed to job knowledge and technical skills, an essential element but not as important as the next characteristic. The study found that 85% of one's success is determined by what they called "ability to deal with people" and "attitude."

MENTAL SNACKS

Quick Rules for Successful Relationships:

1. Make sure you make other people feel important.
2. Remember that a person's name is the sweetest sound in any language.
3. People respond to praise and want to be treated with respect.
4. Continue to work on your communication and relationship skills. (Your ability to work with different personalities will be a key to your future.)

One final thought on people skills:

"Anyone can be polite to a king, but it takes a real person to be polite to a beggar."
—*Jim Shea*

DREAMS

Did you know that when our attitudes outdistance our abilities even the impossible becomes possible? That is why it is important to work on your attitude every day. When you couple a positive attitude with the power of a dream, you position yourself to begin to live your dreams. It works like this:

• A dream without a positive attitude produces a daydreamer.

• A positive attitude without a dream produces a nice person who isn't going anywhere.

• A dream plus a positive attitude produces a person on their way to reaching their potential and all sorts of strong possibilities for their lives and organizations.

To accomplish a lot, to go far in life or to reach your full potential, you need both. I remember a few years ago sitting down one night and journaling. I was in a funk and dissatisfied with my life, yet I had fulfilled most of my goals at 36 that I had written down five years earlier. As I began to pray and look at my goals, it hit me like a ton of bricks. Five years earlier I had dreams and goals that I wanted to achieve. Now I had accomplished them, and I had stopped dreaming. What did I do that night? I began to dream again. I began to write down dreams I had for my marriage, kids, work, career, travel, etc. It ignited the fire inside of me. Here are some questions we need to ask ourselves: Am I dreaming? Do I have the dream for success or have I allowed circumstances or other people to kill my dream? Today, make sure you've written your dreams on paper and are pursuing them with a positive attitude. Nothing can stop the person with the right attitude!

Decisions

Life is a sequence of choices. The decisions you make today will create events in your life tomorrow. If you eat two slices of pecan pie every night, what is the inevitable outcome? If you smoke two packs of cigarettes daily, what is the inevitable eventuality? Everything you are presently doing will affect your present or your future. The choice is yours. You will make many decisions today. Some of them will give you pleasure now, but tomorrow you will be miserable over those decisions. Some of those decisions may make you a little uncomfortable today, but, tomorrow, you will be thrilled. Reprogram your thinking to distance. Reprogram your life for endurance. Patience is powerful. Your decisions today can create the circumstances you desire tomorrow.

> "Half the world is composed of people that have something to say and can't, the other half who have nothing to say and keep on saying it."
>
> —Robert Frost

COMMUNICATION

A legendary management guru once claimed that 60% of all management problems result from faulty communications. This may have been a low percentage when you begin to think about how much people are self-consumed. Make sure you're not so wrapped up in your own life that you forget how to relate to others. Lack of communication is one of the biggest problems you will encounter in life, whether it's your employees, your associates, your boss or even your family. True communication is more than just listening and speaking to someone. It is also being friendly and helpful. (Remember, if you want a friend, be one.) It is also smiling—it takes 72 muscles to frown, only 14 to smile. And it is being generous with praise and cautious with criticism. It is being genuinely interested in people. You can like almost everybody if you try. It is being alert to give service. What counts most in life is what we do for others. Have a good sense of humor, a big dose of patience and a dash of humility, and you'll be rewarded many-fold!

A Moment to Consider

A friend sent me the e-mail below, and it made me double-check my attitude one day. I wanted to share it with you because it reminded me again that everything in life is about attitude and perspective.

One morning a woman woke up, looked in the mirror, and noticed she had only three hairs on her head. "Well," she said, "I think I'll braid my hair today." So she did and she had a wonderful day.

The next day she woke up, looked in the mirror and saw that she had only two hairs on her head. "Hmm," she said, "I think I'll part my hair down the middle today." So she did and she had a grand day.

The next day she woke up, looked in the mirror, and noticed that she had only one hair on her head. "Well," she said, "today I'm going to wear my hair in a pony tail." So she did, and she had a fun, fun day.

MENTAL SNACKS

The next day she woke up, looked in the mirror and noticed that there wasn't a single hair on her head. "Yeah!" she exclaimed, "I don't have to fix my hair today!"

It is important to walk our lives giving thanks in all things. Your attitude and perspective is everything!

CRITICISM VS. CORRECTION

Success is like a blackboard—when you make your mark on the world, watch out for the people with erasers! It really doesn't matter what profession you are in, you are going to meet and be confronted by critics. It has always amazed me that most critics generally have never walked a mile in the shoes of those they criticize. Yet they still don't hesitate to pass harsh words. The fact is, critics are spectators, not players. Critical people are usually disheartened people who have failed to reach a desired goal. Someone once said, "Criticism is the death gargle of a non-achiever." Criticism points out your flaws, but correction points out your potential. Children, relatives, friends and employees need more correction and less criticism. Big difference! There has never been a monument built to a critic. Be aware that the critics are out there. Don't let them hold you back or slow you down!

Where the Rubber Meets the Road

Most people don't realize that successful individuals always face challenges and setbacks before they succeed. One of the biggest challenges you'll have to overcome is the sting of criticism. Whenever you try a new way, dream big or aspire to accomplish more than your friends, family or envious people think you are capable of, just get ready for the opposition.

It was former president Theodore Roosevelt who gave us the best words in defense of the man or woman living where the rubber meets the road. See if you agree:

"It is not the critic who counts, not the man who points out how the strong man stumbled, or where the doer of deeds could have done them better. The credit belongs to the man who is actually in the arena; whose face is marred by dust and sweat and blood; who strives valiantly; who errs and comes short again and again; who knows the great enthusiasm, the great devotions, and spends himself in a worthy cause; who, at best knows in the end the triumph of high achievements; and who at worst, if he fails, at least fails while daring greatly, so that his place shall never be with those cold and timid souls who know neither victory nor defeat."

Remember, nobody ever casts stones at a fruitless tree.

People need MODELS to follow, not mottoes

A blind man in the city was sitting at a street corner with a lantern beside him. A woman passed by, noticed the man and inquired why he had a lantern even though he was blind. The blind man simply replied, "So that no one may stumble over me." He was holding a lantern so others would see him. As a leader or manager in your organization, is your behavior, or are your actions, the example of the behavior you expect from your employees? Leaders in any organization must model the behavior they desire from the rest of the company or team. Whether you're a company executive, teacher, spouse, minister, little league baseball coach, big league player or political leader, the message is the same. Let your lantern burn brightly so others won't stumble. People may doubt what you say, but they will believe what you *do!*

ENCOURAGEMENT

Encouragement is the seed of inspiration. In the early 19th century, a young man in London aspired to be a writer. But everything seemed to be against him. He had not been able to attend school for more than four years. His father had been thrown into jail, and he often knew the pangs of hunger. He got a job in a rat-infested warehouse, and he slept in the slums. He had so little confidence in his writing abilities that he mailed his first manuscript in the dead of the night so nobody would laugh at him. Story after story was refused. One day, one story was finally accepted. True, he wasn't paid a shilling, but one editor did praise him. One editor gave him recognition. Because of the praise, recognition and encouragement of just one person, this young boy was transformed into one of the most noted writers of all time. His name? Charles Dickens. You have the power to encourage, too. Whether it's a child, spouse or employee, nothing stimulates growth so much as praise and encouragement!

Are You Dreaming?

That is not really the question. The question is, "Do you have the courage to act on your dream?" When you dream, you rise above your limitations and you move from where you are to where you want to be or should be. In other words, you begin to see your goals in their completed state. Thoreau said, "It's fine to build castles in the air, so long as you work to put foundations under them."

Today I want to encourage you to keep dreaming and challenge you to pursue those dreams. When you begin to pursue your dream, somebody will always emerge to rob you of it. Is there a dream in your heart? Has life buried it? Have others told you it's too late? Don't believe it. Noah started building the ark when he was 500 years old. Ronald Reagan became president approaching 70 years old. Dr. Robert Lopatin became a doctor in his mid-fifties. And some mothers have gone back to get a college degree after their kids graduated from high school. The point is this:

Keep pursuing your dreams because it is never too late. Dreams are the joy of your present and the hope of your future! Protect your dreams. Feed your dreams. As long as you have a dream you'll never grow old. Two quick thoughts regarding your dreams:

1. **Dreams separate leaders from followers.** The fact is that dreamers are in the minority. Those who live only by what they see will always outnumber those who live by vision, dreams and faith.

2. **Dreams are usually outside the realm of the expected.** In other words, most people will look and say "you've got to be kidding" or "that will never happen."

It is usually a friend or family member who will try and remind you the reasons it won't or can't happen, but don't believe them. All things are possible if you believe and have the courage to pursue your dream!

> "It is what we think we know that prevents us
> from learning something new."
> —Claude Bernard

BE READY

Have you noticed that there are no straight lines between where you are today and your goals? Everything changes. Life happens. You change. That is why the shortest line between you and your goals will always be curved. In other words, there will be plenty of ups and downs in your pursuit of your dreams. The question is only: "How curved will your curve be?" That will all depend on your habits, faith, focus and ability to adapt to change.

We all know that we'll encounter twists and turns in life, but very rarely are we ready to confront them. Think about some of the most exceptional people in their fields like athletes, teachers, firemen and artists. They all spend more time practicing and rehearsing than they do performing. Whereas most people do just the opposite. They spend almost no time planning or practicing but they're always rushing to perform. In the rush to accomplish things, there is little attention to actually learning (in advance) better ways to live and lead. One of the keys to achieving your goals will be to anticipate change. Are you flexible and attentive to those things happening around you? Do you have a teachable spirit or are you a know-it-all? Here are a couple of thoughts to keep in mind as you pursue your goals and confront the curves in life:

1. Listen more and talk less.
2. Hear less and absorb more.
3. Connect more and compete less.
4. Flee less and fight more.
5. Risk more and resist less.
6. Assume less and succeed more!

Failing and Getting Up

Most people who are considered highly successful today have failed far more times than they have "won." The game of baseball is a perfect example: Hank Aaron and Babe Ruth both struck out far more times than

MENTAL SNACKS

they got hits or home runs. Thomas Edison failed at his inventions far more times than he succeeded. It's a well-known fact that Walt Disney, Ray Kroc, Bill Gates and many other successful people struggled. Michael Jordan and Larry Bird both missed more shots than they made. Whether in sports, business or parenting, the fact is, you will fall down many times in life. Successful people fail and make mistakes. However, they never give up. They take responsibility for their actions. They don't blame the past, their family or anyone else. When they fall down, they dust themselves off, get back up and continue to pursue their goals. Do you? Remember, only those who are willing to endure the pain of the struggle will ultimately enjoy the rewards of success!

> "Most stress is caused by people who
> overestimate the importance of their problems."
> —Michael LeBeouf

STRESS

When was the last time you woke up totally refreshed, ready to take on the day? How long did you stay energized and excited about your day's activities? In today's world, the stresses of life have depleted people's ability to do their best, be their best and enjoy the journey of their daily responsibilities and commitments.

Currently, more research is confirming that close to 80% of the illnesses treated in this country are EII (emotionally induced illnesses). This means stress is a primary contributor to sickness, disease and depression.

The word "stress" is used, misused, abused and overused in daily conversations. What is stress? Dr. Hans Seyle, the father of stress management research, defines stress as "the wear and tear on your body caused by life's events." It is the body's physical, mental and chemical reactions to circumstances that frighten, confuse, endanger and irritate. Remember, there is positive stress and negative stress. However, each person must determine what is the right amount of stress for he or she to function at his or her optimum capacity. Too much stress can negatively impact your health. Experiencing too little stress can cause boredom, dullness and apathy. Fortunately, there are plenty of strategies we can practice that can help us keep our lives in balance. Here are a few stress management strategies:

1. **Passionately pursue your purpose.** People who feel a sense of purpose and commitment have a tendency to view obstacles in life more as challenges rather than threats and aren't affected by stress in a negative way. How do you view obstacles to your goals?

2. **Make a plan and work it.** Emotionally and spiritually healthy people tend to maintain a high degree of control over their life. They take one day at a time and choose how they invest and spend their time. What about you?

3. **Put problems in perspective.** The old saying is true, "Everything has a solution except death and taxes." Make sure you don't overestimate your problems.

4. **Change your oil.** Most people take better care of their cars than they do themselves. Work out, eat healthy, relax, laugh, pray and enjoy your life.

5. **Keep life in perspective.** Focus on the positive. Keep failure and mistakes in perspective. Continue to feed your faith and develop your enthusiasm.

Your Body Counts

Many mental factors are involved in being happy and successful. Having a positive attitude, being persistent and setting goals are just a few. However, there is a physical element that is also involved in being happy and successful, and that is your health. The great thing about your health is that you can control it with the habits you keep. You decide whether to exercise or not, whether to eat properly or not. In a study of 7,000 people in Alameda County, California, researchers found that the healthiest people develop seven basic habits: They don't smoke cigarettes, they have regular physical activity, they use alcohol moderately or never, they get 7 to 8 hours of sleep every night, they maintain their proper weight, they eat breakfast and they avoid eating between meals. And remember, a healthy body leads to a healthier mind!

"The human brain is a most unusual instrument
of elegant and as yet unknown capacity."
—Stuart Seaton

PERSEVERANCE

Thomas Edison once said, "Many of life's failures are men who did not realize how close they were to success when they gave up." Walt Disney was actually fired by a newspaper editor who told him, "You're not creative enough!" Richard Bach wrote a story about a seagull and was turned down by 18 different publishers. Undeterred, he kept knocking on doors until finally McMillan published his story. Within five years, *Jonathan Livingston Seagull* had sold more than 7 million copies. Don't ever give up! Perseverance is the power to endure and face defeat without giving up. Successful people realize that rejection or defeat is merely a temporary setback on the way to their goal or dream. The key to persevering is to feed your faith and starve your fear. Both of them will be with you, but the one you act upon will dominate your life. Remember, success and victory go to the people who never give in, never give up and never quit!

Your Brain

The other day in a meeting, I caught myself going on and on to some of my employees that we have to continue to work harder, faster and smarter. After the meeting, I started to reflect on how we can hardly turn around these days without hearing someone talking about taking it to the next level or needing to achieve more results. That got me thinking about the biggest obstacle to accomplishing one's dream, and it happens to be our brains.

Why is it that when people are young, one can sense the hope, aspirations, energy and potential of a person? But as we get older, one can see so much complacency, so much empty striving and so much lack of aspirations all around us. What happened? Most of the time it is the cynical and negative voices that have crept into our brains and planted their seeds. They began to harvest fear-driven and doubt-producing fruit in our minds. We have to fight for our minds. You have to program your brain to think, focus on and meditate on life's possibilities. Then when you align your thinking with your energy and effort, you begin to see results in your business, family and life. Think about it. What happens next in your life is not solely in the hands of fate or the people around you. It is in the power of what you dare to think, imagine and do.

God gave us two ends—one to sit on and one to think with. It is evident that the success or failure of anyone is dependent on which one they use the most. Make sure you use your brain, and use it wisely!

> "The way to accelerate your success is to double your failure rate."
> —Tom Watson, Sr.

FEAR OF FAILURE

As you drive toward your destiny, you'll hit some potholes and occasionally take a few wrong turns. Actually, the only way to avoid failure is to never leave your driveway! The issue is not whether you are going to fail, but whether you're going to learn from it and make it an asset. Are you going to turn it into wisdom to succeed and move forward? In a recent survey of highly successful people, none of them viewed their mistakes as failures. They simply called them "learning experiences," "tuition paid" or "opportunities for growth." The next time you fail at something, ask yourself these questions: "What have I learned?" "How can I turn it into success?" "Where do I go from here?" "How can my experience help others?" "Did I actually fail, or did I just fall short of an unrealistically high goal?" Failure is success if you learn from it!

How Is Your FOF?

Did you know that FOF (Fear of Failure) is one of the primary enemies of you reaching your full potential? FOF is one of the biggest obstacles in the journey of living your dreams. FOF brings fear of taking risks, and you'll never get what you want out of life without taking some risks. Why? Because everything worthwhile in life carries the risk of failure. Failure is nothing more than a natural consequence of trying. Every successful person you have read about, have met or have known has experienced some level of failure. Today, I want to remind you of a couple of important things to keep in mind when you stumble, fall down and experience failure in the pursuit of your goals.

1. **Always keep failure in perspective.** We will never know what we can achieve until we try. If we make a mistake, fall short or mess up, so what? That's why erasers were invented. Keep it all in perspective. Failures are only temporary and only as big as you allow them to become.

2. **Failure gives you an opportunity to start again.** It's like coming up

MENTAL SNACKS

to bat in a game of baseball. If you strike out swinging, you have to put it behind you and get ready for your next time at bat. Once failure is over, forget it and let it die. It's time for a new beginning. Authors Warren Bennis and Bert Nanus, in their book, *Leaders: The Strategies of Taking Charge*, wrote, "Failure is a beginning, the springboard to renewed efforts."

3. **KEEP GOING!** It's a fact and has been quoted by several high achievers but our greatest glory is not in never failing, but in rising every time we fall. History has demonstrated that the biggest achievers and winners in life usually encountered heartbreaking obstacles, defeats and adversity before they succeeded. They finally won because they refused to quit, to be discouraged by their failures. Today, put failure and the past behind you and press on...keep going!

OPTIMISM

Have you ever noticed how everything from the news comes from a pessimistic perspective? Take for instance the person who delivers the weather. The weatherman says, "partly cloudy." Why can't he say, "partly sunny today?" The weatherwoman says, "40% chance of rain." Why can't she say, "60% chance for a sunny day?" You rarely hear positive news or about the people who have overcome adversity and obstacles to succeed. To hear those types of stories you have to hunt them down yourself most of the time.

I want to remind you that no matter how tough things are or how hopeless things look, there is always a way out, if you look long and hard enough for it. Today we need more optimism than ever before. This doesn't mean that we should blind ourselves to reality. We all need to maintain an optimistic outlook regardless of the situation, while at the same time examining it to make sure we're not wearing blinders. Just like the successful executive who asserted that he was very optimistic about the future of the business. A reporter asked him, "Why, then, do you have such a worried look on your face?" The executive replied, "When you're optimistic, it always pays to worry about your optimism."

I learned a long time ago that there is no payoff in staying discouraged. Staying consumed on the negative and cynical side of life never brings any joy or solution to your situation. However, working toward solutions, praying, keeping busy and making optimism a way of life can liberate you from the funk of discouragement and restore confidence in yourself. Eventually, if you don't give up, you will win!

Resistance and Opposition

In 1954, all the leading medical journals said that the four-minute mile was not humanly possible. Doctors warned athletes of the dire consequences of attempting it. Coaches encouraged their runners to do their best but forget about achieving it. However, that same year, Roger Bannister broke the four-minute mile! Forty years later, Eamonn Coghlan of Ireland did it too—at the age of 41. When you begin to believe that you can achieve your goal, you activate motivation, commitment, confidence, concentration and excitement inside of you. Henry Ford was right when he said, "Whether you think you can or you can't, either way you're right." Believing doesn't mean it's going to be easy. The path to personal achievement is uphill all the way. But whether it's athletics, business, sales or academics, keep in mind that airplanes and kites rise faster when they fly into the wind. Remember that you only grow stronger when resistance and opposition test you.

"Whatever you want to accomplish, you must think it, see it, and do it!"
—Anonymous

VISION

It is so critical to have a vision for your life. A vision is no more than having a mental image so sharp and clear that you are able to *picture* something in your mind. It gives meaning to your existence and gives you a reason to get up every morning. A vision for your life also helps you keep fighting against the odds you encounter along the way. It will give you inspiration and motivation to keep striving until you've reached your goals or fulfilled the dreams in your heart.

Having a vision for our lives is like a trail we can follow. The trail may occasionally lead us through dense forests and dry places, but if we stay on track, we eventually reach our destination. What is your vision for your family? What is your vision for your professional life? What is your vision for your finances? What is your vision for your legacy? Maintaining a clear-cut and unambiguous vision is critical to your life. A couple of other thoughts on vision:

1. When you have vision, you have a sense of direction and a reason for living.

2. When you have vision, you become disciplined, empowered and full of energy.

3. When you have vision, you live a meaningful and rewarding life!

Remember, you don't build your future by looking at the past or looking backward. You create your future by vision.

It's Your Time

Did you know the currency of Japan is the yen? The peso is the currency of Mexico. The dollar is the currency of the United States. The currency of life is time! You can be happy and not pay attention to time, but you will not be an achiever. If you are going to succeed in your relationships and career, you have to account for your time. Everyone is given 365 days a year and 24 hours a day. Successful people are different because they accomplish more by managing their priorities, events and opportunities in their time schedule, rather than wasting any of their time. Know the true value of your time. Invest, seize and enjoy every moment. Never put off until tomorrow what you can accomplish today.

> *"Most of our journey in life is learning about and overcoming adversities."*
> —Julio Melara

PERSISTENCE

Did you know that most successes have been built on failures? The majority of all great achievements have been the final result of a persistent battle against discouragement and failure. If you are facing obstacles on your quest for success, or you are coming up against some adversity in pursuit of your goals, understand that you must keep the faith and keep fighting, no matter what. You must persevere!How do you know when you have persevered enough? When you have achieved what you set out to do!In 1905, the University of Bern rejected a Ph.D. dissertation as irrelevant. Albert Einstein was disappointed, but not defeated. He persevered. Michael Jordan was cut from his high school basketball team. Henry Ford went bankrupt twice in his first three years in business. During its first year in business, the Coca-Cola Company sold only 400 Cokes. A football player was told he was too small and too weak to play football. Today, Fran Tarkenton is in the Hall of Fame. You may never make history, become a famous athlete or invent a new product, but whatever your dreams are, never quit!

Expect the Best

You've heard it before, "What you see is what you get." But it should be this: *What you expect is what you get.* Expect great things of yourself. Expect awesome things to happen today. Expect high achievement. Expect the best! The bumblebee doesn't know it is aerodynamically impossible for him to fly. He simply expects it of himself.

What do you expect of yourself? Are you like the bumblebee that doesn't know he can't? Or do you limit yourself by staying within restrictive boundaries? Do you give up too easily? Today I want to challenge you to enlarge your dream and enlarge your expectations. Dr. Denis Waitley wrote, "Make your goals out of reach...but never out of sight." Meggido Message has said, "If you have accomplished all you planned for yourself, you have not planned enough."

Don't limit yourself by planning only that which is possible to accomplish. Think and dream big. Why? Because you can. Expect the best today and for the rest of your life!

Which One Are You Feeding?

A grandfather was talking to his grandson about how he felt, late in life. He said, "I feel as if I have two wolves fighting in my heart. One wolf is full of anger, despair and hopelessness. The other is full of compassion, strength and hope."

The grandson asked, "Which wolf will win this fight in your heart?"

The grandfather answered, "The one that I feed."
—*Unattributed*

"The final test of a leader is what he or she leaves behind
in other people…the conviction and the will to carry on."
—Unknown

LEADERSHIP

Influence cannot be asserted; it can only be earned. If you think you've got the same influence with everybody, try telling your best friend's dog what to do. Influence comes from the time you invest, the interest you show, the consistency you demonstrate, and above all, the trustworthiness you exemplify. In other words, influence comes from having integrity; and nothing is more important to your future than personal integrity. Integrity always puts character over personal gain, people over things, service over power, principle over convenience and the long view over the immediate. This means that if your level of influence has been negative or low, you can change. You can become a person of influence who helps and serves others.

Leadership Is Leading by Example

In Noel Tichy's book *The Leadership Engine*, he writes, "The companies that consistently win don't just have one strong leader or just a few at the top. They have lots of strong leaders, and they have them at all levels of the organization."

Management guru Peter Drucker said, "Leadership is hard work. It is about results, not just efforts. It can be mundane, unromantic and boring. It often has little to do with so-called leadership qualities and even less to do with charisma. Leadership is only a means…to what end is the crucial question."

In other words, the end result of leadership is not about a title, status, position or accomplishments of the leader as much as it is about the accomplishments of the people, team or followers. It is about the direction the people are being led in and *whom* they are becoming in the process. What is your philosophy of leadership? Are you about serving others or just wanting to be served?

Leadership is all about serving and never asking someone to do what you are not willing to do yourself. It is all about being an example to others and assuming responsibility for results that will benefit those being led. Are you an example to your department or organization?

Socrates said a person must first understand himself or herself before being able to make a significant contribution. His advice was "know yourself." Do you know yourself today? Aristotle told his followers that in order to develop their talents and use them for a meaningful purpose, they must "discipline themselves and have direction for their lives." Do you have the discipline and focus required to lead others?

Those are two important concepts that Socrates and Aristotle gave us, but the ultimate given about leadership came from Jesus. His message was not only about knowing yourself or controlling yourself but also about giving yourself and risking the investment of yourself into others. In washing his disciples' feet, he reminded them that no leader is greater than the people he or she leads. Wow! There is the example and challenge of our lives! Remember, to serve is to rule!

SUCCESS IS A JOURNEY

Harvard psychologist William James said, "The greatest discovery of my generation is that a human being can alter his life by altering his attitudes of the mind." Can our lives actually be enhanced by changing our attitudes? You bet! Whether you like it or not, who you become on the outside is who you are in the inside. Attitude is the reflection of a person and your world mirrors your attitude. Author James Allen put it this way: "A person cannot travel within and stand still without." Ultimately, what you experience, achieve or don't achieve depends on your attitude. Few things can stop the person with the right attitude, but nothing can help the one with the wrong attitude. What happens in life happens to all of us. It's not what happens to you that matters. It's what you do with what happens to you that counts!

There Are No Pit Stops

I remember reading a few years ago about one of the greatest virtuosos of all time, Paganini. He performed his first concert at age 11. Ultimately, he revolutionized violin technique forever. When he died in 1840, he bequeathed his violin to his birthplace of Genoa, on one condition: that no one play it ever again. The city fathers agreed and put it on display. But wooden instruments have a certain peculiarity. As long as they're played, they show no wear. But if they lie unused, they begin to decay, which is exactly what happened to Paganini's violin. Other instruments of the same vintage, handed down from one musician to another, continue to bless the world. Unfortunately, Paganini's became a crumbling relic of what it might have been. What a lesson!

Today I want to remind you that success is a continuing journey. It involves growth and development throughout your life. There are no pit stops. Consider these concepts if you want to succeed in all areas of your life:

1. **You lose what you don't use.** Make a commitment to grow daily, and as you do, you will begin to see real change.

2. **Don't wait for inspiration.** Sometimes you can run on enthusiasm, but most of the time, only discipline will carry you through.

3. **Dream big!** Why? Because you can! By thinking of limitations and excuses, you create them. The God-given potential within you is limitless.

4. **Learn to master your time.** Life is filled with critical moments when you trade one thing for another. Always trade up, not down.

> "Wisdom is knowing what to do; virtue is doing it."
> —David Starr Jordan

DON'T GIVE UP!

Many people give up just when they're about to attain success. A high school basketball coach was attempting to motivate his players to persevere through a difficult season. Halfway through the season, he stood before his team and asked, "Did Michael Jordan ever quit?" The team responded, "No!" He yelled, "What about the Wright Brothers? Did they ever give up?" "No!," the team resounded. "Did John Elway ever quit?" Again the team yelled, "No!" "Did Elmer McAllister ever quit?" There was a long silence. Finally, one player was bold enough to ask, "Who's Elmer McAllister? We've never heard of him." The coach snapped back, "Of course you've never heard of him—he quit!" Remember, when you want something you've never had, you've got to do something you've never done. Never give up!

Your Commitment

We're currently going through growing pains in our firm, and as we continue to hire more people and leverage our ideas for growth and service, the responsibility of leadership has never been more clear to me.

True leadership is all about commitment (the promises we make and keep for the benefit of the people in our organizations). Our responsibility is for the long-term benefit, not for our own short-term gain. No company, ministry or team can function to full potential or capacity unless its people can rely on the commitments of their leaders. It is a leader's "word" that provides the framework for relationships and for the organization's growth. We must keep our promises to our employees, employer, families, to all those we lead, even at the expense of risk and sacrifice. That is why being open and transparent generates trust and a reciprocal commitment from those we lead. If you want to build trust and commitment from those you lead, you have to give it away first!

Know What Is Important

The greatest things:
The best day — TODAY
The best policy — HONESTY
The best work — WORK YOU LIKE
The greatest mistake — GIVING UP
The most ridiculous asset — PRIDE
The greatest need — COMMON SENSE
The wisest shortcut — DEVELOP MENTORS
The greatest fault — TO BE AWARE OF NONE
The greatest truth — WE REAP WHAT WE SOW
The best habit — MAKING GOOD ON ALL COMMITMENTS
The best teacher — ONE WHO BRINGS OUT THE BEST IN YOU
The greatest thing in the world — LOVE (Love of family, home, friends, associates, company and country)

> *"One of life's most painful moments comes when we must admit we did not do our homework, that we did not prepare."*
> —Merlin Olsen

BEING A LIFETIME STUDENT

Did you know that you can create a future characterized by high performance and fulfillment by making a lifetime commitment to think right, work right, study right and live right?

Here are three strategies to help you form the habit of studying right:

1. Plan and prepare well. Spectacular performances are always preceded by spectacular preparation. Cultivate the will to plan and prepare.

2. Find a mentor. When selecting a mentor, search for the individual traveling the same road you're traveling and one who is out in front. One whose reputation and achievements you admire and respect.

3. Develop the slight edge. A slight improvement in one skill can do wonders for your performance over a period of time.

Remember, competence never lacks opportunity!

The Ritz Has a Special Touch

I recently spent the weekend driving my wife through parts of New Orleans she had not seen since Hurricane Katrina hit. While we were downtown we stopped in front of the Ritz-Carlton Hotel, and I thought about the magic touch the Ritz-Carlton Hotels have always had. Did you know that in 1983 William B. Johnson purchased the Ritz-Carlton in Boston and purchased the rights to the Ritz-Carlton name? He redefined hospitality in the United States with the Ritz-Carlton luxury setting. This included white tie and apron uniforms for the wait staff, black tie for the maître d' and morning suits for the rest of the staff. In addition to gourmet cuisine, you can find fresh flowers scattered throughout all public areas of the hotel.

There's even a little history behind the Ritz-Carlton logo. The Ritz-

Carlton logo is a combination of a lion and a crown that was originally designed by Cesar Ritz. The primary goal of the Ritz-Carlton Hotel Company is nothing short of 100% customer satisfaction and their commitment to employee training is proof of their commitment. All employees are taught about providing "lateral service" to their co-workers. During the training program all employees are taught that protecting the assets of a Ritz-Carlton Hotel is the responsibility of every employee. All employees carry a laminated card listing the 20 basic keys to the Ritz-Carlton culture and are taught that the proper response to any customer requests is, "Certainly," or "My pleasure." Only 1 of 10 applicants applying for a job at the Ritz-Carlton makes the cut.

Here is the lesson and the challenge: How well are you training your people? What type of plan do you have for professional and personal growth? Are you committed to taking your attitude, your competence, your sales or leadership to the next level? The only thing certain about tomorrow is that it will be different from today. That means you must keep striving for excellence, and you must continue to change if you're going to make the cut!

A LITTLE EXTRA EFFORT

Did you know that both of the premier auto racing events, the Daytona 500 and the Indianapolis 500, take about three to three and a half hours to complete? Here is the amazing fact: In the last 10 years of each race combined, the winner took the checkered flag by an average margin of 1.54 seconds and took home $1,278,813 in first place money. The average prize for second place was $621,321. In 2008, swimmer Michael Phelps became the only person in history to win eight gold medals at a single Olympics. But remember that in the 100-meter butterfly, trailing in the final meters, he unleashed several giant strokes and an extra, little half-stroke to win by a fingernail—one-hundredth of a second. Regardless of whether you're running a business, making a sales call, raising a family or preparing for an exam, it's the extra effort that makes all the difference in the world. Extra ideas on extra effort:

- As a parent, you can add an extra 30 minutes each day to invest time with your children.
- As a salesperson, you can make an extra call or presentation each day or week.
- As a leader, you can take a few extra minutes to acknowledge or recognize valuable employees.
- As a friend, you can choose to visit or talk with one extra friend each week.

The point is obvious. When you put a little extra effort forward, you open up additional opportunities and possibilities in the areas that mean the most to you.

The great Elbert Hubbard once wrote, "The line between failure and success is so fine that we are often on the line and do not know it. How many a man has thrown up his hands at a time when a little more effort, a little more patience, would have achieved success. A little more effort and what seemed hopeless failure may turn to glorious success."

Excellence and Your Effort

So many people are constantly trying to get by with as little effort as possible or settling for less than they are capable of. Yet life only gives back to you what you put into it. (The law of sowing and reaping.) Here are three key thoughts on your journey of excellence and fulfillment:

1. **Consider your commitment.** When you are compelled daily to do everything in your life as well as it can be done, you will touch the borders of excellence. The extra attention and extra effort will always bring you over the top.

2. **Pay the price.** Nothing is free in this world. True excellence does not come cheaply. A certain price must be paid in terms of patience, practice, productivity and persistence.

3. **Never settle for just "good enough."** I like one of Hallmark's long standing slogans, "Hallmark cares enough to send the very best." The question is: How about you? Are you the best? Do you always do your best? Do you believe in always trying your best? Remember, perfection is not the goal but EXCELLENCE is!

"Problems should be utilized. If you've never been unhappy,
how would you know what happy is?"

—Malcolm S. Forbes

SOLVING PROBLEMS

Did you know that you were hired to solve problems? It is one of the greatest ways we bring value to our organizations and customers. Creativity is the search for solutions, and problems are the catalyst for creativity. If you think about any inventor, for instance Thomas Edison, most of his inventions were created to solve an existing problem. Why did you buy your car? It solved a transportation problem. Why do you read magazines or newspapers? They solve information problems. I can look at any profitable business and attribute their success to the problems they solve in the marketplace. Lawyers solve legal problems, mechanics solve car problems, salespeople solve revenue problems, accountants solve tax problems and the list goes on and on. Today, I want to remind you of a few keys to a successful future:

1. The more problems you solve the more you position yourself for promotion and financial rewards. Are you solving enough problems?
2. Somebody needs you today, and I want to challenge you to grasp your significance and value. You are a solution to someone.
3. The day that you begin to cause more problems than you solve, you become dispensable.
4. You'll only be remembered for one of two things in your life—the problems you solve or the ones you create.

A Formula for Leadership

Saturday morning I was having coffee with my buddy, entrepreneur extraordinaire and restaurateur Lou DeAngelo Jr. He started DeAngelo's Pizzeria Company in Baton Rouge, La., in October of 1991 at the age of 19. Lou is a native from Jersey with passion for people and pizza. He began working at the age of 10, washing dishes, bussing tables, working the counter and eventually making pizzas. Today, he has several businesses that generate well over $12 million in revenues and has hundreds of employees. We were talking about leadership and the challenges all leaders go through when he stopped me and shared with me a formula he constantly reviews. A friend shared it with him and I want to share it with you. Here it is:

L = f (s, o, l, f)

What does it mean?

Leadership is a function of: the situation, organization, leader and followers.

In other words, one cannot just come up with a simple formula for being a leader. You can have a great leader and put him or her in a terrible situation and there is no guarantee it will succeed. The opposite is also true. You can have a great organization, but if you put in a bad leader, it won't succeed. The lesson is a great one to remember. You always have to take into account the current situation, the DNA of the organization and mindset of the followers whenever you're looking to hire or promote someone into a leadership position.

"To be good is noble; but to show others how
to be good is nobler and no trouble."
——Mark Twain

SOWING AND REAPING

L istening to many people lately, I have been reminded about how impatient we have become in America. Many people want their "ship to come in" before they have even stepped out and sowed their time, energy or resources. Whether you have an idea like Fred Smith had with Federal Express or Ray Kroc had with McDonald's, every long journey starts with the first small step. In other words, acorns can become oak trees, but you must start with what you have and where you are.

I remember as a student in college, I didn't have money, but I had plenty of time. So I sowed my time and energy and worked two jobs while going to school. Every day I sowed excellence as a courier (just a fancy name back then for gopher) and went above and beyond that call of duty. Do you know what happened next? I got promoted. Don't look at what you don't have, but start using whatever you have in your hand and heart. You have to sow seeds before you can reap anything. A seed is a tiny beginning with a huge future. It is the beginning. A seed is anything you can do, know or possess that can help somebody else. Your time, money, talent, kindness, love, work and patience are all seeds. Anything that improves another person's life or your organization is a seed. Too many people are so busy studying what they don't have that they overlook something they have already received.

Today, I want to challenge you to stop looking at what you do not have, and start focusing on something you've already been given and begin sowing. Your gift, skills or talents can be sown into your colleagues at work, your family at home and your customers in the marketplace. The seeds that you sow today will help create the future you desire!

What Are You Believing?

So many people live in a very restricted circle of their potential because of the way they believe. A big challenge in all of our lives is finding facts we need to know for peak performance and getting rid of myths. Today, I want to challenge what you believe regarding some popular myths on performance and your potential for success. Here are a couple of misconceptions that may be limiting you:

MYTH: Competition is a great thing to have in your organization. It promotes winning and excellence.

FACT: Competition wastes up to 40% of our time and energy and has never promoted excellence. Competition forces us to constantly compare ourselves to others, and we end up in the minutiae of mediocrity or trying to tear down others so we look better. In every field and industry, research shows that star performers have learned that no one has to lose for them to win. Great performers focus their attention, strength and talents on excelling, going above and beyond the best they have ever given before. In other words, they compete against their best!

MYTH: Don't sweat the small stuff, and it's all small stuff.

FACT: It's the little things that make the biggest differences. Our firm recently won a national award for being the best business newspaper in America. I can tell you it is because we do sweat the small stuff that our quality is so good. Some pet peeves and little irritations are worth sweating in work and life because they can turn into huge problems if they are ignored.

Remember to give the world the best you have every day and the best will come back to you!

> "Every production of genius must be a production of enthusiasm."
> —Benjamin Disraeli

THE "WOW" FACTOR

I just got back from a family trip to Disney World. My kids loved it, but mom and dad are worn out! As usual, I was amazed at the "WOW" factor they deliver at all of their amusement parks and special events. Their organized systems and the extraordinary service they deliver are second to none, which is why Mickey Mouse knows how to make money. A couple of quick observations and lessons we can learn from Disney:

1. **Training:** It is obvious they train and teach their employees about service, processes and customer service. That is why they have created an educational institution within their own organization. I found out that they train and remind their employees all about the Disney experience, mission and passion.
Question: How much time and resources are you investing in your people? If the people around you are not growing, the organization will not grow.

2. **Passion:** Everywhere I went, I sensed a deep emotional passion by most of the employees for Disney and the core purpose of the company. I received "good mornings" from not only the characters, but also from the people cutting grass and picking up trash. That passion was evident from the moment we arrived at the hotel and were greeted by bell hops to the moment we checked out. They even told me, "Have a magical day," when I checked out (Believe me, there was nothing magical about the bill!). However, the smiles and passion I sensed left an impression on our family.
Question: How many of your employees have passion? Is the "wow" factor evident to your customers, colleagues and vendors daily? Without passion you have little power to influence.

3. **Core Values:** Somehow they have found a formula for growing their organization and preserving the attributes that led Walt Disney to start the company. It is very challenging to grow a company and do it in a way that preserves your core values and your vision and delivers

MENTAL SNACKS

exceptional quality service consistently all while maintaining a pervading sense of excitement, purpose and direction.

Question: Is your team committed to preserving your core values, and at the same time, highly focusing on growth of the people and company? Does everyone on your team have the fundamentals/basic principles, processes and procedures memorized?

One final observation—after being out since 7 a.m. and returning back to our hotel at 9 p.m. one night, we began to reflect on the day. It was physically, mentally and financially draining. We were so exhausted that we developed a new slogan for Disney: "Disney...where everything is make believe except the cash!" Ha!

As we laughed, and I shared that line with another friend, he reminded me of the best lesson of the whole trip:

Cost to take the family to Disney: EXPENSIVE!

Memories that last forever: PRICELESS!

Serving

We are all familiar with the legendary service and growth of Southwest Airlines. The success and phenomenal growth they have experienced has always been because of the philosophy of their leadership. Here is a mental snack from their former CEO that we all need to remember as we focus on bringing our organizations to the next level:

"The essential difference in service is not machines or things. The essential difference is minds, hearts, spirits and souls."

It's all about the people!

> *"I never remember feeling tired by work,*
> *though idleness exhausts me completely."*
> —Sherlock Holmes to Dr. Watson

EVERY DAY IS A HOLIDAY

Besides speaking and writing, I'm also in the publishing business. One of the cool things about enjoying what you do every day is that you love getting up in the morning and engaging the day's challenges, projects and assignments. Almost daily I remind my employees and colleagues that when you work at the *Business Report*, every day is a holiday! Of course, most chuckle, some disagree and a few agree. It's all a matter of perspective. Too many people in America have become complacent and have a sense of entitlement, not realizing that we are blessed to not only have a job but be able to go to work every day and earn a living.

People quickly forget that when you go to work every day, you're not just making a living, but you are building your life. Unfortunately, those who only look at their work as a means of getting money never really have any at the end of their career. The ancient scripture in Ecclesiastes 3:22 says, "There is nothing better for a person than to rejoice in their work." Do you enjoy what you do daily? Do you celebrate your company and co-workers or just tolerate them? My personal observation over the years is that men and women who get to the top of their field were those who pursue and tackle their assignment with energy, hard work and enthusiasm. It's all about the way you look at your work. So if you need to shift your perspective, read some of these thoughts about work:

1. There are many formulas for success but none of them work unless you do.
2. Work is the least expensive way to occupy your time.
3. Work is the easiest activity a person has to escape boredom.
4. The common denominator for success is work.
5. It's the extra work you do that is the difference between success and failure.

And yes, if you do what you love and you love what you do every day, then every day is a holiday!

"You will never change your life until you
change something you do daily."
—Unknown

GOOD OR BAD HABITS

Did you know that your life is a reflection of your habits? People do not decide their future but decide their habits and their habits decide their future. Successful people simply have great habits. They are willing to do the things average people don't like to do. Today if you're looking to make some changes in your life, then first change your choices, and then you will change your life. Here are some habits you might want to adopt:

- Focus on first things first. Make prioritizing a priority every day.

- Be a finisher. Be known as a person who commits to finishing what you start.

- Get up earlier. The early bird not only gets the worm, but gets a head start on the rest of the world.

- Have breakfast meetings. Get the day off to a good start.

- Stop taking work home with you.

- Read more books and attend more seminars. Become a lifetime student.

- Watch less TV and spend more time communicating and cultivating relationships you value.

- Work out at least three times per week. Take care of your health.

Give Away Ideas

Do you remember in school other students preventing you from seeing their answers by placing their arm around their exercise book or exam paper? It's kind of the same way at most places of business when it comes to ideas and creative solutions. Some say, "Don't tell them the idea, they'll take credit for it."

The problem with hoarding your ideas is you end up living off your reserves and eventually you become stale. If you give away and share your ideas and thoughts, somehow more come back to you. The cool thing about ideas is that they are open knowledge. What I've discovered over the years is that my ideas weren't mine anyway. They are out there floating around, and you just have to have your brain in the right frame of mind to pick them up. So the next time you have an idea, read a great book or have a creative solution to a problem, make sure you share it with others. You never know when you might need one yourself.

Some Wit and Wisdom

"Some people take no mental exercise apart from jumping to conclusions."
—*Harold Acton*

"There are no short cuts to any place worth going."
—*Beverly Sills*

"We don't see things as they are. We see them as we are."
—*Anais Nin*

"If everything seems under control, you're not going fast enough."
—*Mario Andretti*

"If you believe it will work out, you'll see opportunities.
If you believe it won't, you'll see obstacles."
—Jon Alama

TOXIC WORRY

It seems as though there is an epidemic of worry going on in our world. So much so that Dr. Edward Hallowell, the author of the book, *Worry*, estimates that about 65 million Americans will meet the criteria for anxiety disorder at some point in our lifetime. Over half of us are what he calls chronic worriers.

Today I want to help you break the curse of anxiety. There is a great Proverb that says, "An anxious heart weighs down a person." And yet the burden of anxiety offers no benefits and produces nothing positive in our lives. Someone once said that worry is like a rocking chair...it gives you something to do, but you don't go anywhere. One interesting set of statistics delivers the fact that there is nothing we can do about 70% of our worries.

What we worry about:
40% are things that will never happen
30% are about the past—things we can't change
12% are about criticism by others
10% are about health, which by the way, gets worse with stress
8% are about real problems that can be solved

The bottom line is that worry is not only a waste of time, but it is actually bad for us. The physical and emotional damage caused by chronic anxiety is well documented. Many years ago, research from the Mayo Clinic pointed out that worry affects the circulation, the glands, the whole nervous system and profoundly affects the heart. Other research has discovered links between chronic worry and weakened immune systems and cardiovascular disease. The fact is that none of us is wired for worry. Plus, it is common for people who worry all the time to let their imagination get the best of them. This is why truth can be such a powerful antidote to worry. Because so much of toxic worry is based upon exaggeration or misinformation, the truth gives us the check-up we need. Unchecked, worry seeps into our thoughts, poisons our joy and tries to convince us to give up. I want to remind you that while we live in a world that is filled with struggle and real pain, there is a real difference between worrying and being concerned over issues. Here's the difference:

CONCERN	WORRY
Addresses the problem	Obsesses about the problem
Involves a legitimate threat	Is often unfounded and created in the mind
Is specific (one thing)	Is generalized (involves many things)
Looks for solutions	Creates more problems

Three things you can start doing today to conquer worry in your life:

1. **Always do what is right**: A guilty conscience can cause more anxiety than a world of problems.
2. **Work out**: Regular exercise and adequate rest can defuse a lot of worry.
3. **Share your issues**: Talking your fears out with someone often reveals solutions that you couldn't see before.
4. **Pray more and worry less**: Prayer produces results and worry produces nothing!

Cool Thought:
There is nothing we cannot live down, rise above or overcome!

"You can always tell what people
REALLY BELIEVE by their ACTIONS."

——Julio Melara

MOTIVATION

This morning when I woke up at 4:15 a.m., I didn't want to go to the gym. It was cold outside, and I really just wanted to stay in bed! However, I hired a trainer at the beginning of the year because, in January, when I wrote out my goals and visions for this year, I made a commitment to lose 20 lbs. and get back into shape. I've lost 9 lbs. and have 11 more to go. So I called my trainer at 4:30 a.m. and told him I wasn't feeling that great and was not coming when all of a sudden he said, "Quit being a sissy and get to the gym, I'm waiting for you!" Without thinking twice I said, "I'm on my way," and within 10 minutes, I was working out. One hour later, I felt strong and energized!

The episode reminded me that we all need other people to help us on our journey in life. Whether you're in business, ministry, a teacher or professional athlete, no one makes it to the top of their field without the help of others. Seldom does anyone reach their goals without the encouragement, correction, coaching or support of another person. Today I want to remind you that somebody needs you. Your words will motivate someone incapable of seeing what you see. It may be mental, emotional or spiritual qualities inside of you, but somebody needs you today. You're not needed everywhere, but you're needed by somebody. I want to challenge you to look for opportunities to strengthen, encourage and bless others.

Self-Motivation

There are so many myths regarding motivation that I have often thought about writing a book on the subject. In its simplest form, think of motivation this way.

Motivation is to a person what water and sun are to a tree. A tree that gets minimal sun and water may live, but it won't grow. If it gets a little more sun and water than it needs to live, it may grow but not bear much fruit. Only the tree that enjoys an abundance of sun and water will flourish and produce fruit. If you just want to survive professionally, don't bother motivating yourself any more than necessary. But if you want to improve every day to be the best you can be, feed your mind with a daily supply of inspiration and motivation!

Extra Thoughts:
Motivation is not permanent. Neither is bathing. If you bathe every day, you're going to smell good. So make sure you're reading or listening to something motivating or inspirational every day.

Don't ever tell me you "can't"—tell me another way!

Belief

Doubt is deadly! No person can consistently perform in a manner that is inconsistent with the way they see themselves. All the potential you will ever need is inside you. The wealthiest spot on the planet is not in the oil fields of Kuwait or Saudi Arabia, in the gold or diamond mines of South Africa, the uranium mines of the Soviet Union, or the silver mines of Africa. The richest deposits on earth lie a few blocks and miles away from your house in your local cemetery. Buried beneath the soil are dreams that never came to pass, songs that were never sung, inventions that were never designed, books that were never written, paintings that were never painted, visions that never became a reality and purposes that were never fulfilled. Our cemeteries are filled with potential that merely remained potential. Don't let it happen to you!

> "The mind grows by taking in, but the heart grows by giving out."
> —Warren Wiersbe

YOUR DREAM AND HEART

It was Jiminy Crickett from *Pinocchio* who said, "When your heart is in your dream, no request is too extreme." Today, I want to remind you to never allow another person to create your dream, steal your dream or destroy your dream. Our time is limited on this earth, so don't waste it. Don't be trapped by the limited and cynical thinking of others. Don't allow the opinions of others to steal your joy or the inner voice you hear. I grew up with a stuttering problem. I can still remember the pain of other kids ridiculing and making fun of me. But I had a dream to someday be able to speak fluently. So how did I become a professional speaker? I didn't let anyone tell me I couldn't. I had a dream, and I didn't quit until it came to pass. Now I get paid for my passion!Have the courage to follow your heart and pursue your passion.

There's no doubt that as you pray, stick to your commitments and continue to grow and learn, you can live your dreams. One of the keys in your journey is to make sure you are constantly assessing, revising and tailoring your actions on a daily and weekly basis so you can effectively improve yourself and continue to move forward. Four areas to review to continue your progress:

1. **Are you moving beyond old habits?** Do you have a rigid mindset? Do you easily embrace change? Are you developing new positive habits?

2. **Are you constantly re-evaluating your focus?** Can you redirect some of your minutes or hours to have more time with higher priority areas?

3. **Are you giving back?** Did you give your best this day or week (to your company, clients, family or friendships)?

4. **Are you investing your time?** Where can you save more time? What area can you invest more time that will create more results?

Are You Producing Fruit?

I recently pulled out some of my old journals and began reading them. Inside one from the mid 90s, I found notes from a message from Mother Teresa we should never forget. I share it with you, hoping you never stop bearing fruit.

> The fruit of silence is prayer
> The fruit of prayer is faith
> The fruit of faith is love
> The fruit of love is service
> The fruit of service is peace
>   -Mother Teresa

Goals

Did you know 50% of the people you know don't know where they're going? Another 40% will go in any direction they're led. The remaining 10% know where they would like to go, but fewer than half of them will ever pay the price to get there. The great J.C. Penney once said, "Give me a stock clerk with a goal, and I'll give you a man who'll make history. On the other hand, give me a man without a goal, and I'll give you a stock clerk." While you work on your goals, your goals are working on you. What you get by reaching them is not nearly as important as what you become on the way. What are your goals today? Are they clear enough to write down? Strong enough to help you persevere? Valuable enough to make you pay the price? Remember that winners make goals, losers make excuses!

WHAT'S YOUR MINDSET?

Are you open to ideas and new ways of doing things? Do your colleagues at work or friends consider you a person who embraces change? Recently I had a conversation with an employee who has been with me a long time. We have been launching new initiatives in our company and changing lots of things. It was obvious she was struggling with "new" ways of doing things. What became apparent was that the battle was taking place in her mind. One thing I have learned over the years is that if your mind is set, it is very difficult to change it. Let me give you an example.

Christopher Columbus was born in 1451 in Genoa, the son of a wool merchant. Do you know the standard thinking or "mindset" in those days? It was all about how the world was flat. Not too many sailors sailed too far from shore fearing the worst. Columbus' mind was set. It was set for taking risks and exploring new worlds. It was long before Columbus discovered the New World on October 12, 1492. He changed his mindset, and today we still celebrate his courage and discoveries.

What about you? What's your mindset? Today, I want to remind you only one person has the keys to your thoughts and that is you. Put a lid on all negative and limiting thinking. Negative thinking is usually linked to a past experience. So bury the past or it will bury your future. Put all of your energy into today. If you woke up this morning and didn't see your name in the obituary column, you're alive, so make the most of today!

If you want any area of your life to get better it always starts with your mindset. Expect things to get better and they will. If you expect them to get worse they will. Here's your choice: You can expect the best or the worst but you can only choose one.

Thinker vs. Whiner

There are two types of workers in every company. Thinkers and whiners. The whiners are usually smart and hard workers, but when issues pop up at work, the first thing they do is complain. They are great at fault finding and pointing out problems but seldom offer solutions. They are a constant drain of energy to people around them.

Thinkers, on the other hand, come up with ideas. They can see the exact same problems as the whiners, but they have already thought about possible solutions. Here is the lesson for all of us. When you take personal responsibility and are committed to being a positive force in your organization, you enter into the realm of thinker. You become more valuable to your organization and position yourself for promotion and more financial rewards. Are you a thinker or a whiner? Remember, thinkers know it isn't just about thinking—it's about doing!

A Few Thoughts On Thinking:

"You and I are not what we eat; we are what we *think*."
—Walter Anderson, *The Confidence Course*, 1997

"Did you ever stop to think, and forget to start again?"
—*Winnie the Pooh*

"Invest a few moments in thinking. It will pay good interest."
—*Unknown*

"Some people get lost in thought because it's such unfamiliar territory."
—*G. Behn*

"Thinking is like loving and dying. Each of us must do it for himself."
—*Josiah Royce*

"If everyone is thinking alike, then somebody isn't thinking."
—*George S. Patton*

> "If you don't think about the future, you won't have one."
> —Henry Ford

WORK IS A PRIVILEGE

This past week I read *Forbes Magazine's* "'Richest People in the World" issue and after not finding my name on the list, I went straight to work. The article got me thinking about the privilege and gift of work. That's right, work is a gift and a privilege. Whether we find pleasure in our work or whether we find it to be a boring laborious duty depends on our mental attitude toward work.

Fulfillment and joy in life depend on our relationships and accomplishments. When your talent and abilities are developed over time and utilized through your work, you begin to grow in confidence and strength. Our perspective should be one that understands every day we go to work, it's not just about labor, but it's about building our life! Here are a few keys that can help you enjoy and accomplish more at work:

1. **Become known as a problem-solver.** Your rewards in life are determined by the problems you are willing to solve for others. The more problems you solve for your organization, your clients or colleagues, the more you position yourself for financial rewards and promotion.

2. **Learn everything you can about your job and never quit learning.** You must become a life-time student of your industry. Invest the time studying, reading and attending seminars that can enhance your knowledge and competence. The marketplace is changing daily, so you must stay on top of trends and changes. Remember, the person who knows "how" to do a job will always have work. However, the person who knows "why" will always be the boss.

3. **Keep a daily master list of your top priorities.** Guard your focus and time as you focus on these priorities. Remember, you can be happy and not prioritize, but you can't be an achiever. You have to maximize the moments every day to maximize your life.

4. **Do more than is expected of you.** Those who only do the minimum required only get the minimum reward. However, if you want to

experience an abundance of satisfaction and rewards then always go above and beyond the call of duty. This was one of the golden keys my mother gave me as she instilled in us a strong work ethic. She used to tell us to be proactive and do whatever it takes to help the team and get the job done (of course, that was part of her speech on my training ground of doing chores around the house)!

If you focus your life on sowing your time and talents with excellence on the job, then you'll begin to experience enduring success!

Just Work Half a Day

The founder of Holiday Inns, Mr. Kemmons Wilson, was invited to deliver the commencement address to a graduating class at the high school he attended but never graduated from. Wilson began his speech with, "I really don't know why I am here. I never got a degree, and I've only worked half days my entire life. Work half days every day. It doesn't matter which half you work...the first twelve hours or the second twelve hours."

Mr. Wilson's advice may seem a bit demanding, but the reality is that in today's world, there are too many people desperately seeking ways to minimize the hours they work and are expecting high compensation, great perks and privileges in return. The fact is, regardless if you're an attorney, salesperson, minister, soldier or teacher, you have to study, think and work hard. The only easy place in this world is the cemetery. You have to answer for yourself the following questions and there lies the key:

What do you want from your work?
What level of success do you want to achieve?
What price are you willing to pay to make it happen?

Answer these questions and commit to working half days and you're on your way!

LIVING WITH PURPOSE

While preparing for an upcoming talk I was giving in California on the subject of purpose, a thought hit me—life is so full of potential! Life is meant to be lived to the fullest. Many people only experience a fraction of life's potential because they haven't decided what they want or where their life is going. Too many people have the "que sera, sera" syndrome. You've seen it and heard it. Their approach to life is, "I just want to live day by day and see what happens." Well baby, its time to wake up and smell the coffee! A quality life does not happen by chance. A fulfilling life begins with searching for and clarifying our reason for living. In other words, our life's purpose. Today I want to challenge you in this area. Without purpose, an understanding of what we want out of life, we become wandering generalities. Life is too short to waste away just existing.

Below is a starting point to help you gain traction in clarifying your purpose. The list below is not designed to become a "to do" list for you. All it is intended to do is to help you capture a better view of what is possible and meaningful to you. Don't hold back and don't censor yourself. Dream big, have faith and have fun!

1. List the three things you value most in your life.
2. List the three things you need most to improve your life today.
3. List three important things you want to accomplish in the next 12 months.
4. List 10 things you are most proud of about yourself or life to date.
5. What do you believe you are here on the earth to accomplish?
6. What are the top five things that matter most in your life?
7. How do I rank the following in order of priority: (1-6)

_____Family/Relationships
_____Work/Professional career
_____Spiritual connection/My faith
_____Friends/Community

_____Health, well-being/Peace of mind
_____Finances/Financial security

When you finish, keep your answers close to you as they will remind, inspire and motivate you toward what is most important to you this year. Then in January, do this exercise again! Remember, more people will fail because of a lack of purpose than through lack of talent.

A Few Other Thoughts on Purpose

"Purpose is the engine, the power that drives and directs our lives."
—*John Noe*

"Great minds have purposes, others have wishes. Little minds are tamed and subdued by misfortunes, but great minds rise above them."
—*Washington Irving*

"Never work just for money or for power. They won't save your soul or help you sleep at night."
—*Marian Edelman*

"A man who becomes conscious of the responsibility he bears toward a human being who affectionately waits for him, or to an unfinished work, will never be able to throw away his life. He knows the 'why' for his existence, and will be able to bear almost any 'how.'"
—*Victor Frankl*

> "The deepest craving of human nature is the need to feel appreciated."
> —William James

YOU CAN DO IT!

While millions of people on the earth go to bed hungry every night, billions of people go to bed every night hungry for a simple word of encouragement, appreciation or recognition. Someone once said, "We live by encouragement and we die without it—slowly, sadly and angrily." That pretty much sums up the importance of encouragement. What could people accomplish if they only had others around them encouraging and believing in them?

Every day I am reminded that our success as leaders, parents, coaches and friends is dependent on our ability to create an environment that brings out the best in people. Today I want to remind you that all outstanding leaders constantly go out of their way to boost the spirits of their personnel, staff, family or team. It's amazing what people can accomplish if they have others around them encouraging and believing in them. How will you give people courage to do their best today? What are you doing to express your belief in people around you? What specific actions are you taking to recognize people around you? Are you constantly reminding your kids, employees, colleagues or friends that, "You can do it"? Remember, silent encouragement or gratitude isn't much use to anyone.

The V- Formation

When you see geese flying in a "V" formation, you might be interested in knowing what scientists have discovered about why they fly that way. So if you're building a team, here are some key lessons you can share with your teammates.

1. Fact: As each bird flaps its wings, it creates an uplift for the bird immediately following. By flying in a "V" formation, the whole flock adds at least 71% greater flying range than if each bird flew on its own.
   Lesson: People who share a common direction and sense of community can get where they are going quicker and easier because they are traveling on the trust of one another.

2. Fact: Whenever a goose falls out of formation, it suddenly feels the drag and resistance of trying to go it alone and quickly gets back into formation to take advantage of the lifting power of the bird immediately in front.

   Lesson: There is strength, power and safety in numbers when traveling in the same direction with others with whom we share a common goal.

3. Fact: When the lead goose gets tired, he rotates back in the wing and another goose flies point.

   Lesson: Everyone gets fatigued at some point. Others have to be willing to step up to the plate.

4. Fact: The geese honk from behind to encourage those up front to keep up their speed.

   Lesson: Encouragement and affirmation energize the soul.

5. Fact: When a goose gets sick or is wounded and falls out, two geese fall out of formation and follow him down to help and protect him. They stay with him until the crisis resolves, and then they launch out on their own or with another formation to catch up with their group.

   Lesson: We must stand by each other in times of need. We are fortunate that there are more geese in life than turkeys!

KEEP DREAMING

A few years ago, I had the privilege to speak at the National Conference for Texas Roadhouse in California. Not only are they one of the fastest growing steak restaurants in the country, but their obsession with quality and having fun has helped them continue to be a leader in their industry. What got me thinking about dreaming was their conference theme, "Keep the Dream Alive." After discovering that the Texas Roadhouse idea was literally started with a dream by Kent Taylor in 1993 on a paper napkin, it reminded me that everything starts with a dream. Then at the close of the conference, CEO G.J. Hart delivered a great message on dreaming. As I listened, I reminded myself that all of us have dreams, and that in order to live the life we dream of, we must decide upfront what we want, what price we're willing to pay and understand it will take endurance.

Most of us know the story about Walt Disney's dream. But here are some people who also believed in dreams and had the guts to pursue them:

1. After his older brother was shot down and killed in World War II, Dick Clark listened to the radio to ease his painful loneliness. He began dreaming of someday becoming an announcer on his own show. "American Bandstand" was the product of this man's dream.

2. Ski instructor Pete Seibert was considered crazy when he disclosed his dream to start a ski resort. Standing on the summit of a mountain in the Gore Range in Colorado, Seibert finalized a dream he had since age 12 and began the challenge of convincing others that it was possible. Seibert's dream is now a reality called Vail.

3. Two brothers-in-law had a simple dream of making $75 a week. They started their own business that advertised a single product served 31 different ways. Baskin-Robbins Ice Cream was a dream

come true for its founders—as well as ice-cream lovers everywhere.

4. Bank of America exists today because A.G. Giannini dreamed of starting a financial institution that served "the little guy." Although a high school dropout, Giannini believed his concept could become a national bank. By making unheard-of automobile and appliance loans, his dream became a reality by the time of his death in 1949.

5. Living in a government-funded housing project in Pennsylvania, Mike Ditka dreamed of escaping the mines of his home state. Capitalizing on his dream and athletic ability, he achieved notoriety as a pro football player and head coach of the Chicago Bears.

These people testify to the exciting truth that if you have a dream and nurture it, be passionate about it, and act upon it, you can experience the realization of it!

More Thoughts On Dreams:

"Some people dream of success while others wake up and work hard at it."
—*Unknown*

"Happy are those who dream dreams and are ready to pay the price to make them come true."
—*Leon Joseph Cardinal Suenens*

"A goal is a dream with a deadline."
—*Napoleon Hill*

"You are never too old to set another goal or to dream a new dream."
—*Unknown*

> "Good business leaders create a vision, articulate the vision, passionately own the vision and relentlessly drive it to completion."
> —Jack Welch

MORE ON THE "WOW" FACTOR

These last couple of months I've had the privilege of delivering some speeches to some remarkable companies. They were from different industries, but what struck me is that, to differing degrees, they were *all* in touch with the "WOW" Factor.

While there have been many books and articles on what it takes to be a great company that delivers the "WOW" Factor, the ones that stand out usually have three common characteristics. The organizations:

- Have a clear vision
- Are people-focused
- Are culture-obsessed

Add these up and you get the "WOW" Factor:

Clear VISION + PEOPLE-Focused + CULTURE-Obsessed = "WOW" FACTOR!

Many business experts have talked about the "WOW" Factor for years but it was management guru Tom Peters that brought it to the forefront. What is the "WOW" Factor?

The "WOW" Factor is exceeding the expectations of the client.
The "WOW" Factor brings the element of surprise into your business.
The "WOW" Factor yells, "Yo, baby, aren't you glad you are doing business with us?"
The "WOW" Factor is all about experiences and solutions.
The "WOW" Factor creates loyal and lifetime customers!

What are you doing today to deliver the "WOW" Factor in your business? To your clients? The "WOW" Factor goes beyond "lip service" to customer service deeply rooted in creating memorable experiences. It is an essential element of your business strategy to differentiate yourself from your competitors.

When you're committed to delivering the "WOW" Factor, it will energize your organization, rock your marketplace *and* customers. Ultimately, only the companies who deliver the "WOW" Factor consistently will win the hearts and loyalty of their customers.

Loyalty

Once, two men were traveling together when suddenly they spied a bear. Before the bear saw them, one of the men ran to a tree, climbed up and hid. The other man was not nearly as nimble as his companion, so he threw himself to the ground and pretended to be dead. The bear sniffed all around the fellow, as he lay there motionless, holding his breath. Finally, after what seemed like an eternity, the bear went away. The traveler in the tree came down and asked his friend what the bear had whispered to him when he put his mouth in his ear. The second man replied, "He told me to never travel with a friend who will leave at the first sign of danger." The parable of the bear is a lesson for the ages. In business, or with family or friends, success cannot be found unless everyone on the team holds to the principle of loyalty.

> "You've got to go out on a limb sometimes,
> because that's where the fruit is."
> —Will Rogers

RISK-TAKERS

Have you noticed how every time you have an opportunity to grow, step into new territory personally or professionally, get involved in a money-making opportunity, take on a new challenge or are asked to try something new, fear always appears? Today, I want to remind you that as long as you're committed to growing every day and every year of your life, you will always have to confront fear. Isn't that great news?

The fact is fear and growth go together like red beans and rice. Our personal decision to grow will always involve the choice between comfort and risk. Theologian Karl Barth said, "Comfort is one of the great siren calls of our age."

Do you know the name of the best-selling chair in America? La-Z-Boy. Not work-hard-boy. Not take-risk-boy. Not grow-boy-chair. La-Z-Boy. Our society encourages us to immerse ourselves in comfort. Look at the daily messages we're bombarded with in the media. We're constantly hearing voices telling us to take it easy, "veg out," be a couch potato, and just do less. The natural tendency is to seek a world of comfort and predictability. However, every time you resist those voices and plow ahead toward your goals, you're creating a powerful habit. The habit of taking risk! Remember, unless you try to do something beyond what you have already mastered, you will never grow, and if you don't grow, you're really not living!

One of the best ways to continue to grow is to do something at least once a week that you don't want to do. Ouch! That arrow definitely pierces our comfort zone. Remember, champions are people who are willing to do the things losers refuse to do (even when they don't want to). I had a friend ask me the other day, "When do you have the time to read with your demanding schedule at work and responsibilities at home?" I said, "At 4:30 a.m., and right before I go to bed." I asked him, "Do you think I like getting up that early every day?" The truth is that it is the only time

MENTAL SNACKS

I have, so I began to do it, and now it is a habit. You see, as we expand our comfort zone and pay the price, new opportunities appear, ideas evolve and growing becomes exciting. These new things expand us more, and the growth process continues. Beware: You will be tempted to stop or coast. Don't do it. When you work through discomforts, discouragement, temptations and adversity, you will become stronger!

Other Thoughts on Growth and Risk-Taking:

"I worry that our lives are like soap operas. We can go for months and not tune in to them, then six months later we look in and the same stuff is going on."
—*Jane Wagner*

"What you become is far more important than what you get. What you get will be influenced by what you become."
—*Jim Rohn*

"Behold the turtle. He makes progress only when he sticks his neck out."
—*James B. Conant*

"Sometimes not taking a risk is a risk."
—*Unknown*

> "The only exercise some people get is jumping to conclusions, running down their friends, side-stepping responsibility, and pushing their luck!"
> —Unknown

GET GOING!

What's good for the mind, body and spirit and doesn't cost anything? Answer: exercise. With two-thirds of the American population overweight or obese, you'd think more people would do it more often.

While on vacation, I met Dr. Nick Yphantides (yes, he is slightly Greek). He is the guy that weighed 427 lbs. and lost 270 lbs. *all natural*. I had a chance to hear him speak about his incredible journey and his battle against cancer and obesity. Not only was he inspirational, but his passion and drive to help others have led him to come out with his new book, *My Big Fat Greek Diet*. The book is really good and not about a diet but really about a miracle and a change in lifestyle. It reminded me of the importance of exercise, so I'll remind you of some of the benefits too:

1. You'll feel better
2. You'll look better
3. Your mind will be sharper
4. It's a knockout punch to any lethargic feelings
5. You'll be in much better shape as you get older

Some of you may be saying, "I'm just too busy," or, "I have no time for this thing called exercise." Well, imagine you get an e-mail message from your doctor today. It says, "If you don't do 30 minutes of exercise today, you'll be dead at midnight." If that actually happened, wouldn't you find 30 minutes for some exercise?

The fact is if you exercise today, you'll feel better tomorrow. Get going!

Reflecting

I love vacations because it's a time to refresh my soul, refuel my body and reflect on life. While on my trip I had a chance to do a lecture where I spoke about programming our lives for endurance and the long run. To think about the end now, so when we look back at the end of our lives we have no regrets. Today, I want to remind you to think long-term. Think about your legacy. Legacy is not something you leave behind, it is what people remember about you.

In 1888, Alfred Nobel, the Swedish chemist who made his fortune inventing and producing dynamite, had just dropped the newspaper and put his head in his hands. His brother Ludvig had died in France. Unfortunately, he'd just finished reading the obituary in a French newspaper. Here was the kicker—it was his! Not his brother's. The newspaper had confused the brothers. The headline read, "The Merchant of Death is Dead." Alfred Nobel's obituary described a man who had gotten rich by helping people kill one another. It was this obituary that shook Nobel and changed his life. He decided from that day forward to use his wealth to change his legacy. When he finally died in 1896, he left over $9 million to fund awards for people whose work benefited humanity. The awards became known as the Nobel Peace Prize.

Alfred Nobel was able to take advantage of a rare opportunity most of us do not: to look at his life as though it had passed and still have the chance to change it. Before he died he was able to invest his time and treasure in something of lasting value that even today has a positive impact on our world. Lesson for you and I: It's never too late. What do you want to be remembered for? What would you like your co-workers and clients to say at the end of your career? What do you want your legacy to be? Think about it now!

MOTIVATING OTHER PEOPLE

I was having lunch last week with a friend who is also a client, and he asked me a question I hear often from executives, "How can I motivate my employees to do the things I need and want them to do?" The simple answer is always, "You can't."

Over the years I've discovered that true motivation comes from inside, not from external circumstances. In other words, we can motivate people, but we need to first determine what it is that motivates them. Then we can use this knowledge to channel their energy to focus on the company or team goal.

Here are some key thoughts about motivation that may help you in achieving your team goals:

1. **Understand people are already motivated.** Some people are like water in a faucet. They have the motivation; all you have to provide is the opportunity. The water is already motivated to flow. But it doesn't have the opportunity until you open the tap. Others are like mountain streams, which flow swiftly but follow their own channels. One key for those in leadership should be to invest time discovering their motivations and focusing them toward the goals of the company or team.

2. **People do things for their own reasons, not for yours.** People in leadership positions have to show employees what's in it for them when they follow behaviors that benefit the organization. We can show them by using rewards, recognition and appealing to their sense of pride and achievement. If none of these work, you have the wrong person on the team.

3. **The best way to get people to pay attention to you is to pay attention to them**. This means listening to others and not just hearing them. Listening is active; hearing is passive. If you listen to individuals long enough, they'll tell you what their concerns and problems

are. It's very important that leaders listen to their staff and associates. We need to take the time to get to know them, not just by name, but also by their interests and aspirations. It's amazing what you'll learn if you just take the time to listen.

4. **Most people only change when there is enough pain.** When the pain of staying the same becomes greater than the pain of changing, people will change. Remember, you can't change people; you can only change their behaviors. To change behavior, you must change feelings and beliefs. This requires more than training. It requires education. When you train people, you just try to teach them a task. When you educate people, you're dealing with their heads and their hearts. And when you capture their hearts, the sky is the limit!

One last thought by Dr. Robert Schuller:
"All things are possible when…
…I get organized to succeed."
…I get smarter people to help me."
…I get my ego out of the way."
…I'm willing to share the credit."

> "Life is not so much a fight to be fought or a game to be played or a prize to be won. It's more nearly a work to be done and a legacy to be left."
> —William Arthur Ward

YOUR TASK

"Your task is to build a better world," said God.

I answered, "But how? The world is such a big place and so complicated. I'm small and helpless, there is nothing much I can do."

But God in all His wisdom said, "Just build a better you!"

Thousands of years ago, the wisest man who ever lived gave us a piece of advice worth gold. He said, "Be careful how you think; your life is shaped by your thoughts." Today I want to remind you that all achievements begin with thoughts. Thoughts control our actions. Actions determine results! This is why we must decide upfront what we want out of life. Once we identify and define our heart's desire, then we can begin to set our goals, create habits that lead us to those goals, work out an action plan and then just do it!

Below are questions to help you on your journey. If you haven't pondered these questions before, it is a good place to start. If you're like me and have been doing it for a while, then you might want to do a self assessment and recalibrate some areas in your life. (I do this weekly.) Here they are:

1. Are you excited about what you're doing?

2. Are you satisfied with who you're becoming? (Being always comes before doing.) If you want to accomplish great things, you must first become something great.

3. How are you planning to become stronger financially, spiritually and physically?

4. Are you giving more than you're taking? In other words, are you contributing to the well-being of your family, community, church,

       MENTAL SNACKS

company or neighborhood?

5. How do you want to be remembered at the end of your life? What do you want your legacy to be?

Your answers to these questions will affect and impact your life more than any other decisions you make. People throughout the ages who achieved their goals always had a clear sense of where they were going, and it is no different today. You build your future by looking forward and taking on the personal responsibility for your life. Live with no regrets!

Five Keys to Succeeding

1. Be yourself, forget yourself and give of yourself to others. Your talents are to be given away, not to keep for yourself.

2. Count your assets and your blessings every day. Get rid of any self-pity that tries to rise up.

3. Keep your promises.

4. Overwhelm people with your charm and kindness, not your power.

5. Keep trying, keep moving, keep growing, keep learning, keep earning and keep serving!

> "Great listeners generally close more sales, build stronger relationships and make more money than good talkers."
> —Julio Melara

THE POWER OF ASKING

Did you know that listening is more important than talking? All great leaders understand that there is a time to talk and a time to listen. One of the greatest ways to extract relevant data, vital information and connect with people is to ask questions. If you're going to be effective in your work and relationships, you have to interrogate your world and become a better listener. You have to be open to listening to the thoughts, ideas and needs of others. Very few people take the time to listen to others, but it's one of the primary keys to success.

Great leaders are constantly asking questions. But not just any questions. They ask questions that get to the heart of the matter. Questions that are organic in nature and open ended. Why? Because their questions are links to their desired future. There is a reason why doctors ask you, "Where does it hurt?" There is a reason why lawyers question the witnesses. There is a reason why the best sales people ask great questions. Why is this so important you may ask? Because information is the difference between your present and your future.

Today I want to remind you that *asking* is more important than telling.

A - Always
S - Seek
K - Knowledge

Signs of Great Leaders

Wow! The only word to describe a leader's session I went to while visiting Australia. Great communicator, pastor and entrepreneur, T.D. Jakes, has recently come out with his new book, *Repositioning Yourself,* and he shared a few nuggets during a session that I want to share with you.

MENTAL SNACKS

1. **Great leaders are strategic about everything**.
   They have a strategy for their work, their family, their finances, their health, their money and their future. **Lesson for us**: Let's make sure we're being strategic about every phase of our lives—planning, studying, reviewing, revising and tweaking our plans and dreams consistently.

2. **Great leaders have systems for everything.**
   The more you have on your plate and the more people pull on you, the more systems you must have in place. **Lesson for us**: Stop. Take a breather and re-evaluate the systems/processes in your office or department. Is it time to change them? What about your family, car-pools, sports activities, church commitments and other obligations? Is it time to implement a new system at home?

3. **Great leaders understand the power of synergy**.
   Cooperative interaction among people creates an enhanced combined effort. **Lesson for us**: No one makes it to the top of their game or succeeds in business without others contributing their gifts, talents and time to the overall cause or goal. Are you leveraging all the resources around you to make sure your organization is functioning at maximum levels of productivity or impact?

4. **Great leaders understand the seasons in life**.
   Everything in life is about seasons and cycles. Knowing what season you are in positions you to maximize opportunities and helps you not to get frustrated when certain things are not happening. **Lesson for us**: Seasons were given to us for signs. We must recognize what season of life we are in. When winter is approaching you don't go out and plant seeds. When summer arrives you don't pull out your winter coat to wear to work. There is a time to play and a time to work. There is a time to sow and a time to reap. Make sure you recognize the season you are in and are open to change!

> *"Strength does not come from winning. Your struggles develop your strengths. When you go through hardships and decide not to surrender, that is strength."*
> —Arnold Schwarzenegger

IT'S JUST A SEASON

Have you ever had a week where you felt you were fighting at least five Goliaths at a time? It is one thing to fight one or two giants at a time but what do you do when you're facing several battles and obstacles at once? When hardships and trials that test your faith keep popping up all at once (like when it rains, it pours)? This was the type of week I had last week. I felt overwhelmed with several issues involving business, relationships, opportunities and transactions. After spending time in prayer and reflecting on the week, I was reminded that this is just a season.

It is a fact that we all encounter seasons of struggle, trials and hardships. However, we must have the internal fortitude and spend our energy overcoming rather than just enduring unexpected struggles that confront us. The good news is that we can convert these storms of life into the wind beneath our wings. We can move beyond the limits of our past mistakes and enlarge our capacity to grow stronger. All the challenges we confront can be transformed into lessons that help us become more resilient and resourceful moving forward. Here are three things everyone can and must do during seasons of struggle:

1. **We must be relentless, tenacious and committed to being an overcomer.** Winners in life have the mindset that no matter what challenge or obstacle confronts them, they will PREVAIL. That is why we have to program our minds daily to believe, to learn and to grow.

2. **We must be willing to pay the price for our goals in life.** Winners know they must train diligently and prepare. The reason people say life is a marathon is because we must program our lives for the long term. The race of life can be an extremely gratifying one, if we have prepared and developed the talent inside of us. This means keeping the goal in front of you and not quitting until you achieve your dream.

3. **We must value the process.** Understand that the most valuable lessons in life only come from struggle. You have to be willing to rethink, readjust and revise your plans and your strategy as you run the race of life. This means we must be flexible and open to change.

The biggest reminder is that wherever you are today, it is just a season. If you're in a season of struggle, keep fighting because this shall pass soon. If you're in a good season, don't become overconfident because this too shall pass. Everything happens in cycles and seasons and it's up to you to recognize, understand and not get stuck in the season.

Sometimes, struggles are exactly what we need in our life. If we were to go through our life without any obstacles, we would be crippled. We would not be as strong as what we could have been. Give every opportunity a chance, and leave no room for regrets!

> *"If you have time to whine and complain about something,*
> *then you have the time to do something about it."*
> —Anthony J. D'Angelo

TAKING RESPONSIBILITY

Nothing drives me crazy like a constant complainer. I learned years ago that I don't want anyone on our team that is constantly whining and complaining. I believe every organization is looking for individuals who can recognize issues/problems/challenges, *but* bring solutions and ideas to the table. Have you ever been around a family member or co-worker who is constantly complaining? If you have, you know how annoying it gets. After a while you don't even want to be around that person. Over the years I've discovered that the real solution to complaining is personal responsibility. The day you say, "I want to accept more responsibility for everything in my life," is the day your life changes.

Here are some examples of accepting responsibility:

- If there's a problem in the world that bothers me, I'm responsible for fixing it.
- If someone is in need, I'm responsible for helping them.
- If I want something, it's up to me to achieve it.
- If I want certain people in my life, I must attract and invite them to be with me.
- If I don't like my present circumstances, I must change them.

Complaining is simply the denial of personal responsibility. And blame is just another way of excusing yourself from being responsible.

Next time you catch yourself complaining, stop and ask yourself if you want sympathy for creating what you don't want, or do you want congratulations for creating what you do want? Remember, you can overcome anything if you don't bellyache.

Before You Complain...

Recently, my assistant, Shannon, sent me the poem below. I share it with you in hopes that you keep everything in your life in its proper perspective:

Life Is a Gift

Today before you say an unkind word -
Think of someone who can't speak.

Before you complain about the taste of your food –
Think of someone who has nothing to eat.

Before you complain about your husband or wife –
Think of someone who's crying out to God for a companion.

Today before you complain about life –
Think of someone who went too early to heaven.

Before you complain about your children –
Think of someone who desires children but they're barren.

Before you argue about your dirty house someone didn't clean or sweep –
Think of the people who are living in the streets.

Before whining about the distance you drive –
Think of someone who walks the same distance with their feet.

And when you are tired and complain about your job –
Think of the unemployed, the disabled, and those who wish they had your job.

—*Anonymous*

> "Work is either fun or drudgery. It depends on your attitude. I like fun."
> —Colleen Barrett

100 PERCENT

What type of person inspires and motivates you? Usually it's a person who is very passionate about what he or she is doing. They're on fire, and you can tell right off the bat that they are the type of person that gives 100%! We've all heard the term, "giving it 100%" but what does it really mean? What makes 100%? What does it mean to give 100%? What makes up 100% in life? Here's a simple mathematical formula that might answer these questions for all of us:

If you take
A-B-C-D-E-F-G-H-I-J-K-L-M-N-O-P-Q-R-S-T-U-V-W-X-Y-Z

and represent it as
1-2-3-4-5-6-7-8-9-10-11-12-13-14-15-16-17-18-19-20-21-22-23-24-25-26

then

H-A-R-D-W-O-R-K
$8+1+18+4+23+15+18+11 = 98\%$

K-N-O-W-L-E-D-G-E
$11+14+15+23+12+5+4+7+5 = 96\%$

But

A-T-T-I-T-U-D-E
$1+20+20+9+20+21+4+5 = 100\%$

The lesson for all of us is pretty clear. Hard work and knowledge are a prerequisite for success, but without a positive attitude you'll never reach your full potential and be giving your family, your company and your life 100%!

More Thoughts on Attitude:

"Everything can be taken from a man but the last of the human freedoms—to choose one's attitude in any given set of circumstances, to choose one's own way."
—*Victor Frankl*

"The truth is that our finest moments are most likely to occur when we are feeling deeply uncomfortable, unhappy or unfulfilled. For it is only in such moments, propelled by our discomfort, that we are likely to step out of our ruts and start searching for different ways or truer answers."
—*Scott Peck*

"The greatest part of our happiness depends on our dispositions, not our circumstances."
—*Martha Washington*

"Sooner or later, those who win are those who think they can."
—*Richard Bach*

"Courage is contagious. When a brave man takes a stand,
the spines of others are stiffened."
—Billy Graham

COURAGE IS IN YOUR HEART

Have you ever had fear try to jump on you? Have you ever heard voices in your head say, "You're not going to make it?" Nevertheless, you stepped out of your comfort zone and had the courage to take on whatever you were facing. One of the greatest lessons I've discovered over the years is that courage is not the absence of fear; rather it is the ability to take action in the face of fear. Eleanor Roosevelt said, "We gain strength, courage and confidence by every experience in which we stop to look fear in the face."

Today, I want to remind you that courage is like a muscle. The more we exercise it, the stronger it gets. Courage is the enforcing virtue, the one that makes possible all the other virtues common to exceptional leaders: honesty, integrity, confidence, compassion and humility. In short, leaders who lack courage aren't leaders. Without courage, all virtue is fragile—admired, sought after, professed, but held cheaply and surrendered without a fight. Winston Churchill called courage "the first of human qualities…because it guarantees all the others."

If you *do* the thing you think you cannot do, your hope, your dignity and your courage grow stronger. Someday you'll face harder choices that very well might require more courage. And when those moments come and you choose well, your courage will be recognized by those who matter most to you. When your children see you choose and value virtue more than security, they will learn what courage looks like. What are you waiting for? All the courage you need is deep in your heart!

Cool Thoughts on Courage

"Moral cowardice that keeps us from speaking our minds is as dangerous to this country as irresponsible talk. The right way is not always the popular and easy way. Standing for right when it is unpopular is a true test of moral character."
—*Margaret Chase Smith*

"One isn't necessarily born with courage, but one is born with potential. Without courage, we cannot practice any other virtue with consistency. We can't be kind, true, merciful, generous, or honest."
—*Maya Angelou*

"It is not the critic who counts, not the man who points out how the strong man stumbled, or where the doer of deeds could have done better. The credit belongs to the man who is actually in the arena, whose face is marred by dust and sweat and blood, who strives valiantly, who errs and comes short again and again, who knows the great enthusiasms, the great devotions, and spends himself in a worthy cause, who at best knows achievement and who, at the worst, if he fails at least fails while daring greatly so that his place shall never be with those cold and timid souls who know neither victory nor defeat."
—*Theodore Roosevelt*

> ## "Management is doing things right;
> ## leadership is doing the right things."
> —Peter Drucker

STRENGTH AND STABILITY

Recently, a good friend sent me some powerful thoughts on maintaining leadership, strength and stability during tumultuous times. There were 10 of them, but I want to focus on three of them because regardless of what season of life you are in or what you do for a living, they are great advice for leaders in any field. As you read them, ask yourself, "Am I doing that consistently?"

1. **Audit your actions regularly.** Someone is always watching. Even when we think no one is watching, someone is always watching. Are you telling the truth? Are you "fudging" in any areas? Do you have checks and balances in your life? Do you know what you believe and stand for when gray areas pop up in your personal and professional life? Are you authentic? From my perspective, this means being who you are, all the time. The point here is to make sure you are constantly reassessing your motives, decisions, ego and agenda.

2. **Develop keen discernment.** All leaders must develop an early warning system if they expect to endure and win long term. You cannot afford to be ignorant of other peoples' selfish agenda. This is where experience becomes so valuable. You need to make sure you have a team around you that is committed to the purpose and goals of the organization. Discern quickly, not just the ones in the company that add and multiply to the team, but also those who subtract and divide. After you identify the latter, help them or fire them, but don't complain about them.

3. **Guard and maintain your passion.** Passion is what makes you take risks, carries you to the top, helps you go the extra mile and do whatever it takes to achieve your goals. Passion creates fire and provides the fuel you need to overcome all obstacles. If you have ever built a fire, then you know that the tendency of fire is to go out. However, if you want to keep a fire hot, then you need to feed it and protect it. Very few people will help you do that when it comes to your passion.

Never forget there are two kinds of people: fire *lighters*, those who will encourage your dream and keep your fire hot, and fire *fighters*, those who will throw cold water on the fire of passion that burns inside of you. Make sure you have more fire lighters than fire fighters around you!

On a final note, it's important to remember that purpose and passion go hand in hand. To be an effective leader, you must first care. When you care deeply, you have a passion that is more than simply a spark that gets you started; it is the fire inside that will help you endure. It is a commitment so compelling that your whole being—body, mind and spirit—are engaged. A great leader's passion for a higher purpose is always characterized by openness to possibilities and the belief that people want to work and create a better future. Passion plus possibilities gives you courage!

Cool Thoughts on a Leader's Passion:

"There are many things that will catch my eye, but there are only a few that catch my heart. It is those I consider to pursue."
 —*Tim Redmond*

"Be still when you have nothing to say; when genuine passion moves you, say what you've got to say and say it hot."
—*D.H. Lawrence*

"Chase your PASSION, not your pension."
—*Denis Waitley*

> ## "Many of us crucify ourselves between two thieves— regret for the past and fear of the future."
> —Fulton Oursler

LIVE WITH NO REGRETS

Recently, I was fortunate enough to participate in a men's conference at my church. I had the honor of sitting down for a spontaneous Q&A session regarding success and life. One of the questions was, "Let's say it is 40 years later, and your life is over. Some of your friends and family have gathered after the funeral. What do you want them to say about your life? What do you want to be remembered for?" Talk about a heavy-duty question on the spot. Several thoughts hit me at once, and I want to share them with you today.

First, I want my wife to say, "He was a great husband," and our children to say, "There was no other father like ours." I want my friends, relatives, clients, vendors and competitors to say, "Julio gave it everything he had in every area of his life, and he made a positive impact in my life." What about you? What if you're gone? What do you want to be remembered for?

Second, I don't want to have any regrets. I can candidly say that after forgiving my real father and a few others in my life, I live my life with NO regrets. I tell my wife, kids, brother, sister and mom that I love them every day. I give my work and relationships everything I can. Not 80% or 90%, but 100% every day. What about you? Is there someone you need to forgive or is there someone that needs to hear you say, "I love you?" Have you grown in your capacity to forgive and let go? No more bitterness, envy or unforgiveness in your heart. It's important that we live our lives now with no regrets. You and I can't correct every mistake we've made, but we can learn from them and create a better and healthier future.

Third, we must make focus one of our obsessions. We can't allow distractions and information overload to get us off our course. We can't let our eyes rove, our minds wander or our hearts drift away from what the most important thing in our lives is: RELATIONSHIPS. Relationships that matter the most in our lives. Relationships with our family, with friends, at work, at church and in life.

Today, I want to remind you to think long term about everything in your life. I know things get tough from time to time, but if you persevere, you can and will make it through any situation. Make sure you make decisions now that will help you create the life you want down the line. Live your life with no regrets!

Other Thoughts on Regret:

"I would much rather have regrets about not doing what people said than regretting not doing what my heart led me to and wondering what life had been like if I'd just been myself."
-*Brittany Renee*

"If only. Those must be the two saddest words in the world."
-*Mercedes Lackey*

"Regret for the things we did can be tempered by time; it is regret for the things we did not do that is inconsolable."
-*Sydney Smith*

ACKNOWLEDGEMENTS

Everything we achieve in life is a collaborative effort of many people who have contributed to all of our lives. I'd like to say a heartfelt thank you to the following people for their positive impact in my life:

To my wife, Sherry, my best friend in the world. Her patience, love and strength keep me and our family going.

To my friend and business partner, Rolfe McCollister, for your counsel and support of all my projects. Your commitment to excellence inspires me daily.

To my wonderful assistant, Shannon Rasbury, and the important role you played in helping me to organize, summarize, type and retype the many drafts of this book.

To, Hoa Vu, for your creative insight, and Jerry Martin for your sharp eye and editorial expertise.

To my mother—who is my hero, and to my sister and brother for their love and constant support.

To our awesome team at the *Business Report* and *225 Magazine*. All of them are so much more to me than colleagues; their commitment amazes me every day.

To my friend and pastor, Dino Rizzo, who has allowed me the privilege of serving, along with the people of Healing Place Church, in helping the poor, the hurting, the lost and the forgotten. His example continues to be a source of inspiration.

To the brotherhood, you know who you are—because of your love, support, friendship and the laughter we share my life is richer.

INDEX

INDEX